Creative Writing For English as Foreign Language Learners: A Course Book

Debrah Roundy

Xinghua Liu

Cranmore Publications

A catalogue record for this book is available from the British Library

ISBN: 978-1-907962-83-7

Published by Cranmore Publications

www.cranmorepublications.co.uk

Authors

Native of Idaho, **Prof. Debrah Roundy** graduated from BSU with a BA in Elementary Education and has been a special education teacher, a developmental specialist, a school consultant and a Neurolinguist. Her research interest is curriculum development and she created much of the curriculum used in her classroom. She has written a book on Neurolinguistic Programs for special needs and elementary school children called "NLP 4 Me." Debrah currently works as a Foreign Language Expert with BYU China Teacher's Program in Shanghai, China.

Dr. Xinghua Liu is a Lecturer in Applied Linguistics at Shanghai Jiao Tong University, China. His research interests include second language writing, corpus linguistics and systemic functional linguistics. Currently, he works as the Chief Editor of TESOL International Journal (www.tesol-international-journal.com).

Preface

Through our teaching experience in various contexts, we found that English as Foreign Language Learners (EFL) normally practice short English writing (about 100 to 250 words) on given general topics. These school-sponsored writing activities are useful in training EFL students to learn fundamental mechanics of English writing and learn vocabulary and grammar. They are also welcomed as EFL students often have to write similar essays for various high-stake language proficiency tests, nationally and internationally. However, by predominantly focusing on this type of essay writing, students are deprived of the opportunity to explore themselves and the outside world through languages. In this fast developing world, we trust it is equally important to distill the sense of creativity and criticality among young learners during the process of learning a foreign language. That said, we hold it necessary to expose our EFL students to various genres and empower them to write them by themselves.

Creative writing is still an elusive term and there has not been a fixed definition. In our teaching practice, we regard any types of writing as creative writing other than those short essays done within time limit and under a writing instruction. Therefore, creative writing in our teaching curriculum may include obituary, poems and CVs.

This book is a result of our work to create a curriculum for the third-year English majors at a Chinese university. Students are exposed to western writing, poetry, writers and authors in the course of the year. Most writing is centered around themselves and their families to help them focus on things that could not be lifted from the internet or other sources. The second term students learn to put together a business packet with business letters, a curriculum vita and a resume. They learned how to cite sources using the MLA style.

We cannot thank more our students in the writing classes who were always keen to gain knowledge, quick to learn, as well as kind and cooperative. We learned while working with them.

This book is our first attempt to put teaching material in a book format. We will continue working on this project and make additions and revisions which will be considered for the next version of the book. Thus, we sincerely welcome all your comments and suggestions.

Prof. Debrah Roundy (droundynlp@gmail.com)

Dr. Xinghua Liu (liuxinghua@sjtu.edu.cn)

Table of Contents

Introduction 11

Section 1: Lesson Reading

Lesson 1:	Lesson of Introduction	17
Lesson 2:	Character Sketch	19
Lesson 3:	Obituaries	23
Lesson 4:	Giving Directions	27
Lesson 5:	Writing Directions to Do a Thing	29
Lesson 6:	Descriptive Essay	31
Lesson 7:	The Friendly Letter	33
Lesson 8:	Formal Emails	35
Lesson 9:	Western Culture: Halloween	39
Lesson 10:	Poetry	45
Lesson 11:	Writing a Pro/Con Essay	49
Lesson 12:	Copyright Ways and Haiku	56
Lesson 13:	Thanksgiving and a Christmas Carol	60
Lesson 14:	A Christmas Carol and Character Analysis	75
Lesson 15:	A Christmas Carol and Outlines	89
Lesson 16:	A Christmas Carol and Compare and Contrast Essays	107
Lesson 17:	A Christmas Carol and Peer Editing	121
Lesson 18:	A Christmas Carol and Final Review	126

Section 2: Practice for In-Class Writing

Lesson 1:	Lesson of Introduction	129
Lesson 2:	Character Sketch	130
Lesson 3:	Obituaries	131
Lesson 4:	Giving Directions	132
Lesson 5:	Writing Directions to Do a Thing	133
Lesson 6:	Descriptive Essay	134
Lesson 7:	The Friendly Letter	135
Lesson 8:	Formal Emails	136
Lesson 9:	Western Culture: Halloween	137
Lesson 10:	Poetry	138
Lesson 11:	Writing a Pro/Con Essay	139
Lesson 12:	Copyrights	140
Lesson 13:	Thanksgiving and a Christmas Carol	141
Lesson 14:	A Christmas Carol and Character Analysis	142
Lesson 15:	A Christmas Carol and Outlines	143
Lesson 16:	A Christmas Carol and Compare and Contrast Essays	144
Lesson 17:	A Christmas Carol and Peer Editing	145
Lesson 18:	A Christmas Carol and Final Review	146

Section 3: Selected Answers for In-Class Writing

Lesson 1:	Lesson of Introduction	149
Lesson 2:	Character Sketch	150
Lesson 3:	Obituaries	151
Lesson 4:	Giving Directions	152
Lesson 5:	Writing Directions to Do a Thing	153

Lesson 6: Descriptive Essay 154
Lesson 7: The Friendly Letter 155
Lesson 8: Formal Emails 156
Lesson 9: Western Culture: Halloween 157
Lesson 10: Poetry 158
Lesson 11: Writing a Pro/Con Essay 159
Lesson 12: Copyrights 160
Lesson 13: Thanksgiving and a Christmas Carol 161
Lesson 14: A Christmas Carol and Character Analysis 162
Lesson 15: A Christmas Carol and Outlines 163
Lesson 16: A Christmas Carol and Compare and Contrast Essays 164
Lesson 17: A Christmas Carol and Peer Editing 165
Lesson 18: A Christmas Carol and Final Review 166

Sources 169

Introduction to Creative Writing for English as Foreign Language Learners: A Course Book

Purpose

This book is written to assist you, the student, in writing creatively. Lessons are created to use your own experiences and examples from your life and the lives of those around you. As the year progresses you will explore the Neurolinguistic Meta Model to learn to write more concise sentences. In Book 2 you will learn to cite sources and use quotes properly in a document. You will produce a final project demonstrating creativity and basic writing skills.

Classwork

The lessons are divided into two parts. The first part is to be completed in class. With your peers, you will explore quotes and culture, both their own and other cultures. You will show you know common errors by finding mistakes in a paragraph or other writing. Additionally you will expand a phrase into a sentence, become famiiar with common English idioms, learn about the Neurolinguistic (NLP) meta model and use it to make your writing more concise and learn to cite common sources quickly to help you with future term papers.

The second part of the lesson will be homework. You will have something to write each week. Usually it will be based on a personal experience. Each week will include a short reading on the topic of the week, and later on the idiom and meta model pattern you will be working with in class.

Peer editing is an important part of writing in the western culture. Students support and help each other grow. As you edit you sharpen their skills at finding common mistakes. This will help in your own writing as you become more cognizant of common errors. You will also read other's work and get to know them better. People are so interesting. Soon you will find that you will look eagerly forward to reading and proofing the work of others. It is necessary to bring a colored pen or pencil every week for peer editing.

Your teacher will decide whether to allow you to use their electronic gadgets or not.

Discuss it

For the "Discuss It" section you will have a famous quote or a challenge to discuss from your own perspective. You will use a personal example from your own life or the life of someone you know personally to illustrate or tell about the quote. You may not substitute a quote of your own liking. You will not use the quote or any other quote in your essay. The teacher wants to see your writing only. The essay is to be timed for five minutes. Then you will count the number of words written. Count words even if they are mistakes for we are looking for the number of words. Do not stop to use white out on a timed writing, simply cross out the mistakes and move on. Then you can count the words even though they are crossed out. It is motivating to see how much quicker and deeper you can write as the term progresses and you become more fluent in writing in English. Your teacher may give you one minute before starting to collect your thoughts.

When the five minutes are up, write how many words were written in five minutes, then, if your teacher chooses, you may have 5 minutes more to finish your essay. This should not be a long essay.

Fix It

This task assesses basic spelling, punctuation and capitalization skills. Later in the term it may access skills at citing sources, English fluency and similar skills. The skills assessed are often taken from the previous lesson. These skills are chosen from basic skills and from skills that are commonly missed by EFL learners. You will find it interesting to see how many common mistakes you will soon be catching as your awareness increases. Often there is more than one way to fix the task. There may be a suggested number of mistakes but that is only suggested to give you an idea of how many mistakes you are looking for.

Expand It

Take a simple phrase or sentence and make it bigger by adding to its meaning. It is to be only one sentence long. NO MORE! NO LESS!

The chart below will give you an idea of what your teacher might look for in grading this portion of the class work.

a boy ran	
0	a woman fast.
	Either student did not do the sentence or did not understand the assignment.
1-2	a litle boy walked
	Sentence is expanded very little and/or there are numerous errors. There is no creativity shown.
3-5	The little boy walked to the store
	The sentences is expanded very little or the expansion lacks creativity. There are numerous errors.
6-8	The little boy who lives next door to me walked happlily to the store.
	The sentence show some good expansion and contains no more than two errors.
9-10	The cute little boy who lives next door to me in the green house walked happily to the store this morning to get her mother some fruit for breakfast.
	The sentence is expanded creatively and has no more than one error.

Challenge It

Into your reading you will be given common Meta model "challenges." These come from the study of Neurolinguistic Programs. Although these are really not always violations, they are words that are often not clear to the reader. This will help you, the student, write more concisely so the reading audience can understand more clearly what is written.

Practice Section

In the practice section there are exercises you may choose to do on your own that will be similar to the ones you will get in class. These are for you if you would like to practice. At the end of the section is an answer key.

Tests/Final

The final test is taken from and laid out as the daily work is. There is a sample at the end of the section.

You should keep your class papers to help study.

Section 1
Lesson Reading

Lesson 1: Lesson of Introduction

Homework Assignment

Write a 1-300 word essay about yourself.

Weekly Reading

For your first assignment the teacher would like to see what you already know and what you need to work on. This book will not give you a reading lesson. The assignment is to write an essay about yourself. It should be 100 -300 words long. Your teacher will look forward to reading your essays and learning a little bit about who you are. Please type your essay with double space, and print it out.

Lesson Notes for the student

This may be the beginning of your writing in western style. Much university writing is done using the Modern Language Association (MLA) style. Here is an introduction to the MLA style you will be using for your work. It is good to familiarize yourself with MLA style as it is used for documents in many businesses. Here is an example of what your essay may look like when you are finished. Read the sample for there is important information in it to help you be successful.

Student 1

Name

Student number

Date or assignment

Title

Skip a line and then start your essay. A good essay introducing you will have several paragraphs. There may be two or three. You might tell a bit about yourself and your hometown in the first paragraph. The second paragraph may tell an interesting fact about yourself, why you are here or something interesting that you do. Your third paragraph will pull everything together to make a final document that is interesting.

Do not skip lines between paragraphs in an essay. You will learn more about this later this year. Do double space, however.

If you follow these MLA guidelines your essay should look good. When it is completed, proof read it and look for errors. Next print it out to hand in. Check the printed copy. Sometimes computer in different countries have different formats and your essay may not print out like you made the document look. If this happens to you make sure you write a note to the teacher and tell her what the problem is so that the teacher will know that you know what is wrong. You can download free programs on line that will help you. Open Office is one of those programs.

Heading 1 inch

At ½ inch put your last name and page number for a longer essay

Your information goes on the top and is double spaced

Next the title. It is normally capitalized.

Skip a line and then start your essay. Indent the first word in every paragraph.

Do not skip a line between each paragraph. My computer will not let me do that. If it happens just put a note on your paper.

Remember 1 inch margins around your paper. You can do it MLA.

Assignment Sample.

Professor Roundy
123456789
Lesson 1
267 words

Professor Roundy

Hi, I am having a wonderful time exploring China. My name is Professor Debrah Roundy and my Chinese name is Rong DaiJia (教授荣黛佳). Please call me Professor. Why am I in China? I retired from teaching school in Rupert, Idaho, USA several years ago. I did not want to sit and get old, I wanted to make the world a better place. I found out about a group called BYU China Teachers out of Brigham Young University in Provo, Utah, USA. BYU places retired teachers from the USA and Canada in China to teach English. We are also to learn more about China and tell the people at home when we get back. It is a cultural exchange.

This sounded like just the thing Mr. Roundy and I wanted to do so we signed up. We are glad we did. We found out the students from Jiao Tong University are very good. They strive to come to class on time and get their assignments done. They work hard because they want to have a good future. It has been a wonderful experience meeting so many highly motivated students that we wanted to return a second year and we are glad we did.

We enjoyed it so much we have signed up for a third year, but this time at Tongji University. We will explore a different part of Shanghai while we are here and enjoy sharing culture with our students at Tongji. We really can make a difference. Will you be a student who works with us to make a difference in your life?

Remember to bring a colored pen or pencil next week and every week for peer editing.

Lesson 2: Character Sketch

Homework Assignment.

Write a character sketch about a friend or family member. It should be someone you know personally. It should have 3-5 paragraphs. It should be 1-300 words long.

If you use any quotes, you will need to cite the source.

Weekly Reading

Assignment Sample.

Professor Roundy
1234567890
Assignment 2
388 Words

The World Will be Her Oyster

Do miracles happen? Well, maybe they do. In 2012 I signed up to go to China. My daughter Alyssa was due to have a baby on the day we were to leave. I would not get to see her. I was so disappointed but we could not change the day to go to China as we had to be here to teach and school does not wait for a baby.

I decided to go and visit Alyssa before I left. She lived clear across the USA in Maryland and we live in Idaho. I made the ticket for August 27th. I would fly out, stay five days and then leave for Idaho, then China a half day later.

On August 25th I got an excited call from Alan, Alyssa's husband. Alyssa was having the baby. She was coming early. Her name would be Chloe Jeanne.

On August 27th I flew out to Maryland just as planned. Alan went to the hospital to pick up Alyssa and dear little Chloe. Then we went to the airport to pick me up. We all took Chloe home to their little home in Maryland.

For five days I got to spoil little Chloe and her mother. I held Chloe and took a lot of pictures. I helped her mother by changing the bed and preparing the meals. I cleaned the house before I left. It was hard to say goodbye, but I knew I could see her often on SKYPE.

When we came home from Shanghai to Idaho, Chloe and her parents met us at the airport. They had moved to Idaho to live in our house while we are gone because we decided to come to China again. Our students work so hard and we are proud of the things they will accomplish. They are such good people.

Now I am enjoying little Chloe. She can walk. I was there the day she became a walker. One day she was toddling along trying not to fall. Then she stopped. She got up her courage. She straightened her back. She had made the change in just a few seconds from crawler to walker.

I hope Chloe grows up to be like my students, hardworking and diligent. When she does, as the idiom means, the world will be her oyster.

Reading: A Character Sketch

A character sketch is an essay that paints a picture of someone using words. It is a way to put people on paper and make them real. Character sketches use a lot of descriptive words as colorful paint. Compare the two sentences below.

- Chloe is a little girl.
- With soft brown hair and a quick smile, Chloe is a beautiful little girl.

Using descriptive words makes a sentence more interesting as it paints a picture of the person being written about.

Your assignment this week is to write a character sketch about someone you know well. It may be a family member or a friend.

Your character sketch may have some or all of these parts. The order may vary depending on what you want to say.

Title	A good title is only a few words long but it is catchy to capture your attention so others will want to read what you have written.
Opening	Introduce your topic, the person you are going to write about.
Introduction	How did you meet, why do you know each other.
Description	A physical description of the person, what does s/he look like? What makes them unique, voice, clothes, mannerisms and etc.?
Personality trait	What is a special personality trait this person possesses and why?
Closing	A good closing will tie the essay together and refer back to the opening.

It is time to get started on your essay. Think of the person you will write about. It must be someone you know. What color is his/her hair and eyes? What kind of clothing does s/he like to wear? What is s/he good at? What are his/her dreams? Does s/he like sports or music? Does s/he excel in a particular class in school? Has something unusual happened in his/her life? Think of many things and then start to create and paint a masterpiece of your friend. Below is an essay about my friend. (Note on the title: Salt is very valuable and you will die if you do not have salt in your body. A person who is referred to a salt of the earth is a person who is valuable to the others, valuable to society, often in a quiet way.)

Professor Roundy
1234567890
Assignment 2
<u>354 Words</u>

Salt of the Earth

When I was a young teacher in Parma, Idaho, I rented an upstairs apartment from a little old lady named Peggy Musty. Peggy was an interesting gal and we got to know her a bit. After I got married she would give Mr. Roundy a bowl of ice cream when he got home because she liked having a man around the house.

Often Peggy would tell us about her friend Mabel who lived next door. Mabel was a bit crazy she would tell us. Now we would say that she had Alzheimer's or dementia. But this was a while ago. Peggy would occasionally mention that she had taken breakfast or dinner over to Mabel or had done some financial business for Mabel making sure the bills were paid. I knew that Peggy watched for Mabel and cared for her but I never knew the full extent of it.

It was the first day of school after winter holidays in January 1977 and it was the year of the big snow. There was so much snow that school was cancelled and the entire little town shut down. I lived across from the school and so I pulled on boots and a heavy coat to slog my way across the street just in case some children did not get the word that school had been canceled. Sure enough, there were one or two and I brought them in, warmed them up, and called their families before sending them back home. Finally I slogged back to the apartment and rushed up the back stairs. As I did, I turned and looked at the almost pristine snow. Not entirely pristine? No. There, going to Mabel's house, were tiny foot prints, Peggy's foot prints. Even though the snow was deep and the day was bitter cold, Peggy had twice waded through the snow to make certain Mabel had something to eat and to be ok.

I think it was then that I learned that she loved her neighbor and cared for her. That day I learned what Peggy was made of, the salt of the earth!

Character Sketch: Editing

When you finish your character sketch you will edit it. You should check your writing for punctuation, capitalization, indentation, spelling, grammar, and sentence errors. Also check the formatting of the paper. This is particularly important in eastern countries where computer formats can vary greatly from the common western formats. Ask a friend to read and peer edit it so see that is flows well in English.

Here are some things to watch for:

1. Punctuation

- Does each sentence have correct end punctuation?
- Do I use commas after introductory word groups and between items in a series?
- Do I use apostrophes to show possession?

2. Capitalization

- Does each sentence start with a capital letter?
- Have I watched for capitalization errors my spell-checker might miss?

3. Spelling

- Have I used my spell-checker?
- Have I watched for spelling errors my spell-checker might miss?
- Have I checked the spelling of all names?

4. Grammar

- Have I used the grammar checker?
- Have I checked for easily confused words (to, too, two)?

5. Sentence Errors

- Have I checked for fragments?
- Have I checked for run-on sentences?
- Have I checked for rambling (run on) sentences?

6. Indentation

- Each new paragraph should be indented about 5 spaces.
- This is the standard for the class.
- In other classes and in business letters you may instead skip a line at the end of each paragraph.

Peer editing can make a huge difference especially as you learn what mistakes to pick out. As you and your peer edit your essays you will each become better writers. Next, print out your paper and then look for computer formatting errors. Fix those and you are ready to hand in your essay.

Lesson 3: Obituaries

Homework Assignment

- Write an imaginary obituary.
- It is you 100 years from now (-10 points if not 100 years from now).
- You died of old age, happy in your home (-10 if not happy in home) (-10 if not of old age).
- Use information you have such as the schools you have attended.
- Dream up things you think you will do in your life. Dream big. Your dreams may come true.
- Make it concise, 3 paragraphs and 100-300 words.
- Fill in a chart about how much your obituary would cost.

How much will your obituary cost?	
Word count: how many words	
$0.25 for each word. (WC x .25 = ?)	$
Picture? $100 each	$
Total your family will pay	$

Weekly Reading - How to Write an Obituary

Sometimes people in the United States say, "Remember the Dash." Or "It's all about the dash." What does that mean? When people die, their names are carved into a tomb stone as a memory of their life. Underneath the name is their birth date followed by a dash and then their death date. The dash represents their entire life, the time period between the birth date and the death date, the dash.

An obituary documents the deceased person's life, the dash. It informs people of the death and gives information about planned funeral and memorial services. The obituary demonstrates respect and honor for those who have passed away (died), while informing those who remain of his or her death. Since you will be writing an obituary, here is a guide for you.

There are two kinds of obituaries in the United States of America. These two types are:

1 -- Short and concise. This is often called a death notice.
2 -- Longer and more detailed.

Type 1 is a short notice of death. It's often used for poor people whose family cannot afford an obituary.

Type 2 -- Longer and more detailed

The second type of obituary will create a longer life sketch of the individual who has passed away which may contain several paragraphs. This is typically the type of obituary that is used in funeral programs, prayer cards and funeral keepsakes. It may include the following information:

- Date of birth, place of birth
- Date of death, place of death
- Circumstances of death (This section is optional, and may be general or specific. Rather than referring directly to cancer or Alzheimer's, it may be more appropriate to refer to a "prolonged illness." In cases of suicide, perhaps no information is necessary or given).
- Plans for the viewing (if applicable) and the memorial service
- Name of high school or college from which he/she attended or graduated
- Military service and decorations
- Religious affiliation, such as church or synagogue
- Jobs held - including retirement
- Names and relations of family members, both surviving and pre-deceased, to include parents, siblings, spouse, children, stepchildren, grandchildren, and great-grandchildren
- Awards/Recognitions received
- Organizations to which the deceased belonged (volunteer work, fraternal organizations, veterans' groups, religious orders)

A picture may or may not be included with the obituary. Some families choose a recent picture while others use a picture from an earlier time in the deceased's life when he or she was younger, perhaps from high school, marriage, or the military. Some obituaries have both. The goal is to honor their memory in the most fitting manner.

IN LOVING MEMORY OF

CLARICE LARSON

Born October 31, 1907, at Grace, Idaho

Passed Away November 10, 1993, at Idaho Falls, Idaho

Family Prayer by N. Keith Larson (Son)

SERVICES HELD AT THE
Idaho Falls LDS 9th Ward Chapel
Idaho Falls, Idaho
Monday, November 15, 1993, at 11:00 a.m.
Bishop Romney Painter, Officiating

Prelude & Postlude Music .... Eleanor Hopkins
Vocal Duet .... *"His Eye Is On The Sparrow"*
Joy Nielsen & Jane Magill, Accompanied by Jeff Covert
Invocation .... Carlos Roundy (Grandson)
Life Sketch ...... Debrah Roundy (Granddaughter)
Speaker .... T. D. Madison
Remarks .... Bishop Romney Painter
Vocal Duet .... *"How Great Thou Art"*
Joy Nielsen & Jane Magill, Accompanied by Jeff Covert
Benediction .... Jack Cragun (Son-In-Law)
Dedicatory Prayer .... Donald F. Larson (Son)

INTERMENT
Fielding Memorial Park

PALLBEARERS - GRANDSONS
Clifford Larson, Don Larson
Roger Hoffman, David Crossley, David Larson
Jeff Larson, Carlos Roundy, Kevin Meldrum
Scott Killian, Rich McIsaac

HONORARY PALLBEARERS
Michael Larson, R. Dix Hoffman, Jack Cragun
Pat Larson, 9th Ward High Priests Group

FLORAL ARRANGEMENTS
9th Ward Relief Society Presidency

FLORAL BEARERS
Granddaughters & Relief Society Members

Your kind expression of sympathy and caring is more deeply appreciated than words of thanks can ever express.
The Family of Clarice Larson

WOOD FUNERAL HOME - DIRECTORS

- Write a short imaginary obituary.
- It is you 100 years from now (you will be about 120 years old).
- You died of old age, happy in your home. (The teacher will take off points if you put something else. The teacher wants you to grow really old and pass on happily in your own home.)

- Use information you have, such as the school you attended.
- Make up things you think you will do in your life. Dream big.
- Make it concise, 3 paragraphs and 1-300 words.
- If you are not comfortable writing about yourself, talk to your teacher.

In the United States families are often charged money to put the obituary in the newspaper. They must pay by the word, therefore the obituary must be concise. Count your words when you are done. Each word costs $0.25. To add a picture may be $100 - $150. At the end put how much your obituary would cost.

Sample

Professor Roundy
1234567890
Lesson 3 Obituary

In Loving Memory

Debrah Larson Roundy (7/19/1952 – 7/19/2072) has departed this earth and gone to live with her ancestors and the God she loves. Debrah was the daughter of N. Keith and Bonne Jeanne Evans Larson. She grew up in Boise, Idaho, USA. Upon graduation from Boise State University she accepted a teaching assignment at Parma Idaho where she taught for three years. Debrah later returned to school and got her M. Ed. in 2000 from the University of Idaho. She also earned her Master and Master Trainer, and Global Trainer at NLPU in Neurolinguistics.

Debrah married Carlos Gordon Roundy December 27, 1975 and they made their home in Rupert, Idaho, USA. Together they had five children, Shadrach Allen Roundy (deceased), Seresa Wayment (Todd Wayment, Burley Idaho); Joshua David Roundy, (Tiffany Yost, Rexburg, Idaho); Samuel Hans Roundy (Amy Roundy, Nampa, Idaho) and Alyssa Bonne Slater, (Alan Slater, Rupert, Idaho).

Debrah was active all her life in her church. She served as a teacher, Scout leader, activities committee chairman, newsletter chairman and as singles adult advisor in Shanghai, China. Later in life she and her husband worked in a temple serving others.

Debrah had a private kindergarten, Busy Bee Kindergarten, in Rupert Idaho. Then when kindergarten was put in the public schools she completed her public school career in Rupert, Idaho where she taught special needs children for 15 years. Debrah also worked as a librarian, and as a counselor for exchange students with the AYUSA program. She worked with the BSA program for 34 years and assignments

included Cub Scout Camp Program Director, the Boy Scout Camp Cook, District Commissioner two terms, Round Table Chairman, Activities Chairman and any other position that needed filled. After retirement she and her husband accepted professorships with Jiao Tong University and later with Tongji University working with BYU China Teachers. They especially enjoyed their years in Shanghai with some of the brightest students of China. Leaving China after several years they served humanitarian missions in various parts of the world striving to make the world a better place by sharing their skills learned from a lifetime of service. Debrah participated in many community plays. She was the Local Program Coordinator for the Minico Spuds Special Olympics team for many years. She also spent years working with the Mini-Cassia Christmas Council and the Mini-Cassia Tree Festival. Debrah was honored by the Boy Scouts of America with the District Award of Merit (1976) and the Silver Beaver (1978). She also was honored for her work with youth with the Idaho Brightest Stars Award (2008) and the Jefferson Award. Debrah then returned to their home in Rupert with her husband and spent the last years of her life enjoying her posterity and a lovely garden. She passed away at her home peacefully in her sleep with her loving family nearby on July 19, 2072 on her 120 birthday. The family remembers her as an active part of the world with the motto to make the world a better place, and indeed she did.	
Word Count	**500**
$0.25 for each word. (WC x .25 = ?)	**$125.00**
Picture? $100 each	**$200.00**
Total your family will pay	**$325.00**

Lesson 4: Giving Directions

Homework Assignment

Choose a place in the town where you go to school. Write directions to get somewhere from the main gate of your school to a place you think others would like to go. Make the directions clear and easy to understand. Use walking, a city bus or the Metro as most college students do not have a lot of money. Do not go to a web site that has directions and cut and paste. That is plagiarism and will get you a "0%". Do it yourself. Write as if the person has never been there. Your directions should be about 100-300 words. Who knows, your teacher may follow your directions and see something new. Maybe one of you will collect the directions and post them on the school web site for others.

Weekly Reading – How to Give Written Directions

Have you ever been given directions that were not good? The summer of 2014 I went to the campus of the University of California Santa Cruz to a workshop on Neurolinguistic Programs. I wanted to keep up my skills with the latest learning and information in my field.

That year we were on a new campus. We got directions from the Campus Conference Center. They were not good directions and many people got lost. The directions did not tell what road to turn on. It did not give us any idea of how far to go before we turned. It did not tell us up hill or downhill, left or right. By the time we arrived at the college we were frustrated.

When you give someone written directions it is important that the directions be accurate and easy to follow. The reader is trusting you to get them to someplace they do not yet know how to get to. Think of directions as a series of steps to be followed. What is the first step, the second step, and so on? Put yourself in the position of the person who has never been that way before. What will they need to get where they are going? Providing directions that are brief yet complete makes the travel easier and allows your reader to arrive at their destination without frustration.

Here are some guidelines for you.

- Start with a starting point that is familiar or easy to follow. Write, for example, "From I25 and 15th St., follow 15th St. east."
- Use action words like walk, drive, turn, and exit.
- Give your reader directions such as north, south, right, left, uphill and downhill. Be aware of things people may not know. For instance, if you live in Idaho you may not know which way north or south is. In Shanghai, China it is easy to know as the street signs have the cardinal directions written on them.
- List your directions as the traveler will arrive at each location. Write, "1. Take Snowyville Road, south from the parking lot. "2. Turn left from Snowyville on to Autumn Ave."
- Make it clear which way to turn. "If you are traveling south on Snowyville, turn left on to Autumn Ave."
- Provide the exact address of the place the person is to go and add notable land marks to help them. For example, "2. Turn left from Autumn Ave, at the Bank of America. You will start to go up a hill."
- Provide a contact number to help the reader in case s/he gets confused.

Professor Roundy
October 13, 2015
Lesson 4 Directions
<u>260 words</u>

Driving to The Theater in Rupert

1. Start at a house in Rupert, Idaho, USA. The address is 402 East 16th Street. You will walk or drive as there is no public transportation in Rupert, Idaho. There are only 5,000 people in the town
2. Leave the house and go to the road. It is East 16th Street.
3. Turn to your right. Walk to the end of the street, 3 blocks.
4. You will be at A Street. Turn to your left. Walk south 8 blocks to 8th Street.
5. At A Street turn to your right and cross the road. Walk 5 blocks to F Street.
6. At F Street turn to your left. The post office is on this corner. Walk past the post office 2 blocks to 6th Street.
7. You will pass the fire station. It is a red brick building on the left side of the road. It is on the same side as the theater. Cross the road so you can walk by the theater.
8. You are there. The Historic Wilson Theater is located at the corner of 6th and F Streets. It is at the corner of the downtown Rupert Square. There is a small park and a kiosk there with information about the history of the theater and the Rupert area. Maybe you will see a play, a variety show or a melodrama. It is a central meeting place in Rupert.
9. If you get lost, give me a call at 208-123-4567. I will be glad to help you out.

My house in Rupert, Idaho, USA

The historic Wilson Theater in Rupert,Id., USA

Lesson 5: Writing Directions to Do a Thing

Homework Assignment

Choose something you can do that you can write directions for. It could be simple like tying a shoe or crossing a street or something that you do well. Think of the reader and be creative. Write directions as if someone does not know how to do this thing. Your directions should be clear and concise with only the words needed.

Weekly Reading

Directions on how to write directions.

1. Prepare your document with a heading and margins.

2. Pick a subject. Choose something you like to do such as cooking something, playing a game or sport, doing a craft. What will your audience enjoy? I, your author, can remember directions a fellow student gave in class more than fifty years ago. It was to make aebleskivers, a light, fluffy Danish pancake. We enjoyed learning about a favorite Danish food. Think of something that is a part of your culture that the teacher may not know about. He or she may remember it for years to come.

3. Write the directions. Use words that show order in time such as first, second, next, after that, and last. Often students of English do not know whether to use last or lastly. They are not used in the same way. You usually use *last* to say that an event is the final one in a series of similar events. You use *lastly* when the events are not similar. For example, 'Erica texted her girlfriend last', that means that Erica texted several people and her girlfriend was the last one. If you say instead, 'Lastly Erica phoned her girlfriend', you mean that Erica had done several things and the last thing she did was to text her girlfriend. You can always use last. Lastly have more rules to its use.

   If you prefer, you can number your directions.

4. Check your directions. Did you include all of your steps and are they in the right order?

5. Check for errors. Watch for punctuation, capitalization, spelling and fluency.

6. Print out your directions.

7. Hand your directions in.

Sample of written directions to write an e-mail:

Professor Roundy

October 11, 2013

Lesson 4 Directions

132 words

Sending an Email to Your Teacher

1. Open your internet browser.

2. Open your e-mail program such as yahoo.com, gmail.com or qq.com

3. Click on the new button. It will open up a new blank e-mail.

4. Type in professor@college.edu.com in the **To** line.

5. Go to the subject line and click. Then write your English name, your student number, L-4, and the time your class begins such as 8 am or 10 am.

6. Write the e-mail. Make certain you put a short greeting at the beginning to be polite. At the end put a short closing and sign your name.

7. Go back and check your e-mail for mistakes. You may want to use spell check.

8. Now your e-mail is ready to send. Go to the top and press the send button. Voila! Your e-mail is on its way.

Lesson 6: Descriptive Essay

Homework Assignment

Write a 1-300 word essay about your hometown. This is to be a descriptive essay so describe something with words that paint a picture.

If you have your own picture of what you choose to write about, please add it to your essay to make it more interesting.

Weekly Reading

1. Writing about your hometown in a short essay could be overwhelming. Follow these steps. Write a few ideas down as you go along.
2. Introductory paragraph. Some people like to start with a few facts. You might tell the location and the size of your town. A few facts about your home town makes a good introductory paragraph. Go to the internet and find some interesting facts. Write down the facts you might use.
3. Essay body. Look at the big picture. This is only a 1-300 word essay. You could write an entire book about your hometown. See your hometown in your mind's eye. What is interesting to you? Where would you take a visitor? Write down a few ideas.
4. Closing. Now think about a closing paragraph. How will you pull your whole essay together? Again jot (write down) down a few ideas.
5. Now look at your ideas for the facts. Choose just a few that would be interesting. Most people do not enjoy a long list of facts. Instead choose a few facts that help create a picture of your hometown.
6. Next look at your ideas of interesting places in your hometown. Choose one thing to center the next paragraph or paragraphs on.
7. After this think about how you can tie all of your paragraphs together. Think of it as if you are convincing people to go visit and wrap all of the things together. Eliminate the other ideas you have so you are ready to start writing.
8. Start writing your paragraphs. As you write you may find your essay changes and evolves. It is fun to watch yourself create.
9. When you are done, look at the whole essay as a big picture. What is a title that would be good? Put the title at the top. Center it and capitalize the important words.
10. Now look at the small details. Go back and edit looking for mistakes. If you have a friend who can peer edit it, share with your friend. Make sure your name, student number and other items the teacher may require are on the document in the correct place.
11. Print out your document and hand it in on time.

How to correctly do a title? Writing titles seems to be tricky, even for the native English speaker. Here are some helps so you can be successful.

Write your essay first. As people write, the essay often evolves and in the end it may be a completely different essay than it started out being.

A title needs to be specific. A title such as "Symbolism," "Death", or "My Town" is too vague. You want a title that tells the reader a little about what the essay is about.

Read your essay and look to see if there is a phrase that stands out as a central theme. Often a phrase from the conclusion will stand out and make a nice circle from the beginning to the end.

If you have used a quote for your essay, you may find a phrase in the quote will perfectly illustrate your essay.

For a short essay, a short title is appropriate. You may want a longer title for a thesis or formal research paper.

Unless it is important, avoid using "you," "us," "we," or "I" in a title.

Capitalization is important. Here are some basic rules using the MLA style.

- Capitalize the first word of a title
- Capitalize all proper noun
- Capitalize the last word in a title
- Capitalize all of the nouns, pronouns, verbs, adjectives and subordinating conjunctions (because, although, before, when, as, since, while, if)
- Use lower case for articles (an, a, the)
- Use lower case for coordinating conjunctions (for, so, and, yet, or, nor, but, for, yet)
- Use lower case for prepositions (above, below, on, to, throughout, by, for, in, out, till, up, upon)

Sample Writing

A Great Place to Live

I live in a very small town in Idaho right in the middle of the desert. You may wonder what a small town is in the United States. We have only 5,000 people in our town. Most of the people in our area are farmers and grow things like sugar beets, beans and the world famous Idaho potato. Because it is a desert with only 10 inches of rain a year, we irrigate our land by bringing in water from the river by canals.

Maybe a best loved feature of our city is the Rupert Square. It is a block square park in the center of the town with most of the major businesses lining the street. When the city was first started in 1906 the people built a well. Everyone went to the well to get their water. People would come in to town two or three times a week to get water and they would talk and the children would play. It became a gathering place and eventually a park was made there. The square is covered with many different kinds of trees. Some reach majestically up to the sky hoping to be covered with lights during the cold Christmas season while others reach out their branches to provide a welcome green shade during the hot summer days when gatherings are held.

Each corner of the square is decorated. In the southwest corner is a map of Idaho outlined in stones and filled with colorful flowers. The northwest corner boosts a waterfall with benches for people to relax at. In the northeast corner is a small forest of evergreen trees with a stone bench to sit on and a special black wrought-iron lover's bench where a boy and girl can meet and talk sweet words hidden in the trees. In the southeast corner is a wooden gazebo where programs are held. Often its pillars are festoon in red, white and blue ribbons for patriotic programs are held where the people celebrate their love for our country.

Even though it is a small town, Rupert is a fun place to live in. It is near good biking, boating, hiking skiing, fishing and boating. The people are very friendly and look out for each other. Having a beautiful town square, the people often enjoy opportunities to associate with each other. With parades, celebrations, and town-wide parties, people use the square often and enjoy it fully. It is great to live in a small town Rupert surrounded by friends and people who care. I hope you get to visit someday, I'll take you to the square.

Lesson 7: The Friendly Letter

Homework Assignment

Write a letter to someone you treasure or love. It could be your grandmother or grandfather, mother or father or a teacher you appreciate. Remember a time when this person did something nice for you. Mention it in the letter and say thank you.

Weekly Reading

Friendly letters are almost a thing of the past as e-mail takes the place of a lot of informal communication. Still it is good to know how to do a proper friendly letter as they can come in handy. If someone gives you a gift it is always best to handwrite an informal letter of thanks. Also sometimes it can be romantic to send a letter to someone you love or admire. Follow the steps below for the friendly letter.

402 East 16 Street
Rupert, Id. 83350
October 18, 2014
Space

Dearest Grandma,
space
indent I want to write you a letter just because I love you and I miss you. I know that you are no longer here on earth but my love for you is still alive.

indent You were a good grandma. You did many things for me. I remember when I was six and had to go to the hospital. You came because my mother had just given birth to my baby sister and could not care for me in the hospital. It made me feel so special to have you care for me.

indent Many years passed and I was going get married. I did not feel like I was ready until I brought my special boyfriend to your home so you could meet and approve of him. Of course you did approve of him and that made me feel good. You were married to Grandpa for 49 years when he died.

indent I was so glad I got to say goodbye to you before you died. I hope you are happy now where you are. You were a good grandma and I still love you and appreciate all you did for me.

2 spaces

My Love,

Your little Debby

Sample assignment

Street address

City, State and zip code

Month day, year

Dear Name,

This is where we write the body of the letter. Skip a line after the salutation.The first line of every paragraph is indented. Usually indent five spaces. Skip a line between each paragraph.

When you start another paragraph always skip a line, and then indent. After the last paragraph, skip a line again before you add the closing. If you add a PS., skip a line again.

What is this thing called a P.S. It is a post script. Long ago when paper was very expensive and it took a long time to write and send a letter, the writer might take several days to handwrite a letter. Then after the letter was signed the writer might have something else to add to the letter. When letters were handwritten and in ink, you could not go back and add something to the body of the letter so you added it as a postscript or P.S. If more was added later they writer would add a P.P.S., and if more after that, a P.P.P.S. and so on.

Yours,

Signature

P.S. Add a post script here if you left something out of the body of the letter.

Lesson 8: Formal Emails

Homework Assignment

Write an email to Professor Roundy inviting him to an on-campus event. It can be real or imagined. Make certain you include directions for the building you choose it to be in.

Weekly Reading

In this age of modern technology it is still important to maintain a sense of respect in emails to people older than us or who are our superiors in a business situation. Students who have spent their lives around the internet texting, tweeting and sending emails tend to be brief and may cover a lot in a short period of time.

There are times when a more formal email is needed, for instance when you are communicating to an older person, when thanking someone for a gift or something nice they did, or when communicating with your boss or another superior at work. Today we will explore a formal email.

1. It is wise to have a business email address if your usual address is informal such as hunkman@cheesyname.com. An email address that uses just your name, maybe with underscores periods or hyphens looks much more businesslike.
2. Put something pertinent in the subject line. It should reflect the content of your email. The subject should make it easy for a business wo/man to find the email he needs in a crowded box, for example, "Meeting notes for March 7", or "Bid for Express Enterprises". Keep the subject line short and to the point.
3. When people write to a friend they usually just get right into what they want to say. In a formal email start with Dear followed by the person's title, last name and comma. Example titles include Mr. .Mr. s., Ms., and Doc. Use the last name unless you know a person well and are on a first name basis. If you do not know the name of the person you are writing to use Dear Sir or Madam: and a colon.
4. Introduce yourself in the first paragraph. Add how you got the person's e-mail address and the opportunity you are writing about.
5. In the next paragraph/s write the actual message. Be succinct. If it is long and fluffed up with unimportant details the reader may just give it a glance and miss the message all together. If your message is long, break it up into paragraphs by topic. Put a line space between each paragraph. Do not bother to indent as indenting may be lost during the email transfer across cyberspace.
6. Be sure to avoid informal writing, slang and poor English. Do not use texting or IM'ing words. They are not formal.
7. Use a formal closing such as Cordially, Respectfully, Sincerely, or Best. Follow it with a comma.
8. Sign your full name. If you have a job title that is relevant to the email you are writing include that in the line after your name and write the company name or website in the line after that. If you have your own blog or website that is related to the content of the email, include the link below your name. If the email is about a job, only include career-related blogs or websites, not hobbies or interests. This may mean going to your settings menu in your email program and taking your normal signature off the email.

9. Proofread your email. Check it for spelling and grammar errors. Many email programs have a spell checker. If yours does not, cut your email out, put it in a program such as "word" and let it spell check for you. Fix the errors and paste it back into the email. If this is a very important email, take the time to read it out loud or, better yet, to a friend, and make sure it sounds good.
10. When you are sure it is done well, press the send box. You may want to BCC yourself so you will have a copy for your records.

Here is an example of an email:

To: Earl Corless@edu.com

BBC: Me@edu.com

Subject: Internship for fall

Dear Mr. Corless,

My name is John Doe and I am in your Conversational English Class. It sure is an interesting class and I am glad I have taken it. I actually had a conversation with a student from Australia last week and it was invigoration.

I am contacting you invite you to an on-campus event that will happen next week. I am overseeing it as the Secretary over Competition for our Student Union. We are having a student talent competition and we would like to invite you to be a judge.

If you can attend it will be held in the North Auditorium. To get there from the main gate just go three blocks down Center Avenue and turn to your right at North College. It is on the corner of Center Avenue and North College. It is the four story building on your left with a large glass front and a beautiful chandelier inside that is lit on the evenings of events. The talent competition will be in the main auditorium and the judges will sit on the front row. We will supply the judges with water, forms to fill out on each contestant and a college logo pen that will be yours to keep after the competition as a souvenir.

Please let me know if you can be there. Either email or call me at 204-336-1234. If I do not answer please leave me a text message and I will text or call back.

Thank you for your consideration. It would be a great pleasure to have you at the talent competition and the students would certainly appreciate your time and efforts to be there for them.

Cordially Yours,

John Doe

Student, BYU in Provo, Utah

Meta Model Challenge

You may not have heard of the Meta Model before but the Meta model is a secret to clear and well written writing. These Meta Model challenge words come from the work of John Grinder and Richard Bandler who developed the study of Neurolinguistic Programs (NLP). These are words that are often not clear to the reader. Learning to identify meta model patterns and clarify them helps eradicaate ambiquities in your writing. Words that can miscommunicate, limit, or confuse the reader are discoved and changed so the reader can understand the meaning the writer wants to convey. This will help you, the writer, write more concisely so the reading audience can understand more clearly what is written.

There are 13 commonly accepted meta Model patterns. They are:

Challenge	Brief Description
Model Operators of necessity	Must, should, need, have to, necessary, could
Model Operators of possibility	Can't, impossible, won't, couldn't,
Universal Qualifiers	Always, never, all, every, no one, everyone
Deletions	Omits which, how, when
Unspecified referential Index	Fuzzy noun or object. It, they, this, people, him
Lost Performative	Lost who? Says who? According to whom?
Unspecified Verbs	Vague, generalizing verbs (exercise? Jog or swim)
Nominalizations	Verbs frozen into nouns (can you put it in a wheelbarrow?)
Presuppositions	X is assumed true so Y is also true
Mind Reading	Crystal ball (I know you aren't happy)
Cause/effect	X makes me Y When X then Y happens
I don't know	I don't know
Complex Equivalent	2 different things are stated to be the same

For the rest of the book we will address different patterns, learn to identify them and to change them to make your writing more clear to the reader. Next week in your class work you will have introduced a Meta Model Challenge: Model Operators Necessity.

- Model operators of necessity include must, should, need, have to, necessary, could.
- Your job will be to challenge the Meta model Language pattern.
- Sample. You must eat an orange every day to be healthy.

6 possible challenge answers.

1. If I don't eat an orange every day can I still be healthy?
2. Must I eat an orange, could I eat an apple instead?
3. Why must I eat an orange, I am allergic to them.
4. I do not like oranges, must I eat an orange.
5. Could I drink a glass of orange juice instead?
6. What would happen if I don't?

Often writers say that we must do something but it is really not necessary, it is a choice. Even if it is necessary the reason for the necessity should be given to gain reader "buy in." Buy in means the reader understands the reason or "buys in" to the concept. Take this for an example: "You should save your papers."

Challenge Question: Why should we save our papers?

Expanded sentence: You should save your daily class papers for the entire term because the final test will be taken from your papers.

The teacher wants you to buy in to saving the papers by telling you why. It will be beneficial to you because it will save you study time as your final test will be taken from the concepts on your daily papers.

In some of your lessons you will be asked to write a challenge question. In others you will be asked to expand the sentence with an answer. Soon you will recognize meta model challenges and self-expand them in your writing.

Lesson 9: Western Culture: Halloween

Homework Assignment

You will write rhyming words for some common autumn season and Halloween words. Also you will write a simple poem of 4-8 lines about Halloween, or the autumn season and use rhyming words at the end of each line. To meet the requirements the poem needs to have a rhythm like a song.

If you do not have an autumn season your teacher may assign you another topic such as a holiday you have recently had or one coming up, or use your imagination.

Weekly Reading

HISTORY OF HALLOWEEN

By Debrah Roundy
Pictures from Microsoft Clip Art

Halloween is a minor holiday celebrated on the night of October 31. A minor holiday means that students do not get out of school and businesses continue their usual work for the day. Traditional activities include trick-or-treating, bonfires, parties, dressing in costumes, visiting "haunted houses" and carving jack-o-lanterns.

Irish and Scottish immigrants carried versions of the tradition to North America in the nineteenth century. Other western countries embraced the holiday in the late twentieth century including Ireland, the United States, Canada, Puerto Rico and the United Kingdom, Australia and New Zealand. Through exposure to US television and other media, trick-or-treating has started to occur among children in many parts of Europe, and in the Saudi Aramco camps of Dhahran, Akaria compounds and RasTanura in Saudi Arabia. The most significant growth — and resistance is in the United Kingdom, where the police have threatened to prosecute parents who allow their children to carry out the "trick" element.

Halloween has its origins in the ancient Celtic festival known as Samhain (pronounced "sah-win"), a harvest celebration. The ancient Gaels believed that on October 31, the boundaries between the worlds of the living and the dead overlapped and the deceased would come back to life and cause havoc such as sickness or damaged crops. Therefore the festival would frequently involve bonfires to scare them away. It is believed that the fires attracted insects to the area which then attracted bats to eat the insects. These are additional attributes of the history of Halloween.

Trick-or-treating, is a popular activity for children on or around Halloween. Children go from door to door in costumes, asking for treats. They knock on the door and say out, "Trick or treat?" The "trick" part of "trick or treat" is a threat to play a trick on the homeowner or his property if no treat is given. Trick-or-treating is one of the main traditions of Halloween. It has become socially expected that if one lives in a neighborhood with children one should purchase treats such as small candy, pencils or some small trinket in preparation for trick-or-treaters.

The practice of begging door to door for treats on holidays goes back to the Middle Ages, and includes Christmas caroling (going house to house singing songs and hoping to get a bit of money from the people). Trick-or-treating resembles the late medieval practice of "souling," when poor folk would go door to door on Hallowmas (November 1), receiving food in return for prayers for the dead on All Souls Day (November 2). It originated in Ireland and Britain, although similar practices for the souls of the dead were found as far south as Italy. Shakespeare mentions the practice in his comedy The Two Gentlemen of Verona (1593), when Speed accuses his master of "puling [whimpering, whining], like a beggar at Hallowmas."

Souling appears to be entirely European and was never practiced in America, and trick-or-treating may have developed in America independent of any Irish or British customs. In the histories of Halloween there is no documentation of wearing masks or costumes on Halloween in Ireland, the UK, or America before 1900. The earliest known reference to trick or treating on Halloween in English speaking North America occurs in 1911 when a newspaper in Kingston, Ontario, near the border of upstate New York, reported that it was normal for the smaller children to go street disguised on Halloween in the early evening between 6 and 7 p.m., visiting shops and neighbors to be rewarded with nuts and candies for their rhymes and songs. Later, in 1915, and 1920 there were more newspapers going westward in the USA again reporting on children going trick or treating. The thousands of Halloween postcards produced between the turn of the 20th century and the 1920s commonly show children but do not depict trick-or-treating. Ruth Edna Kelley, in her 1919 history of the holiday, The Book of Hallowe'en, makes no mention of such a custom in the chapter "Hallowe'en in America." It does not seem to have become a widespread practice until the 1930s.The term "trick or treat" first appeared in print in 1934, followed by the first use in a national publication occurring in 1939. In the 1930's costumes for children begin to be sold in stores but most children used an old sheet or their parent's old clothes for dress up.

Although a quarter million Scots-Irish immigrated to America between 1717 and 1770, the Irish Potato Famine brought almost a million immigrants in 1845–1849, and British and Irish immigration to America peaked in the 1880s, yet trick or treating on Halloween was virtually unknown in America until generations later, likely growing quickly because of commercial exploitation. In its' infancy trick or treating was commercially a time to make money selling candy. Later, especially after WWII, the production of costumes begin to grow. By the 1990's the commercial aspects had grown to adult costumes and party supplies.

Early national attention to trick-or-treating was given in the October 1947 issues of the children's magazines Jack and Jill and Children's Activities, and by Halloween episodes of the network radio programs The Baby Snooks Show in 1946, and The Jack Benny Show and The Adventures of Ozzie and Harriet in 1948. The custom had become firmly established in popular culture by 1952, when Walt Disney portrayed it in the cartoon Trick or Treat, Ozzie and Harriet were besieged by trick-or-treaters on an episode of their television show, and UNICEF first conducted a national campaign for children to raise funds for the charity while trick-or-treating.

Although some popular histories of Halloween have characterized trick-or-treating as an adult invention to rechannel Halloween activities away from vandalism, nothing in the historical record supports this theory. To the contrary, adults, as reported in newspapers from the mid-1930s to the mid-1950s, typically saw it as a form of extortion, with reactions ranging from bemused indulgence to anger. Likewise, as portrayed on radio shows, children would have to explain what trick-or-treating was to puzzled adults, and not the other way around. Sometimes even the children protested: for Halloween 1948, members of the Madison Square Boys Club in New York City carried a parade banner that read "American Boys Don't Beg."

A jack-o'-lantern (sometimes also spelled Jack O'Lantern) is typically a carved pumpkin, however apples, gourds and even turnips have been used. Typically the top is cut off, and the inside flesh then scooped out. An image, usually a face, is carved onto the outside surface, and the lid replaced. During the night, a candle is placed inside to illuminate the face with a spooky, eerie glow. The term is not particularly common outside North America, although the practice of carving lanterns for Halloween is.

In folklore, an old Irish folk tale tells of Jack, a lazy yet shrewd farmer who uses a cross to trap the Devil. The devil is not supposed to be able to go in front of a cross for the cross in Christian lore stands for Jesus' willingness of one to sacrifice all for the good of others, and for goodness. One story says that Jack tricked the Devil into climbing an apple tree, and once he was up there Jack quickly placed crosses around the trunk or carved a cross into the bark, so that the Devil couldn't get down.

Despite the colorful legends, the term jack-o'-lantern originally meant a night watchman, or man with a lantern, with the earliest known use in the mid-17th century.

What sets Halloween costumes apart from costumes for other celebrations or days of dressing up is that they are often designed to imitate supernatural and scary beings. Costumes are traditionally those of monsters such as vampires, ghosts, skeletons, witches, and devils. There are also costumes of pop culture figures like presidents, or film, television, and cartoon characters. Another popular trend is for women (and in some cases, men) to use Halloween as an excuse to wear particularly revealing costumes, showing off more skin than would be socially acceptable otherwise.

My fondest memories of Halloween are dressing up in old clothes and carrying a big pillowcase to be filled with candy as we went door to door. We would never play tricks but greet neighbors with a cheery, "trick or treat." When I was in the 5th and 6th grades my sisters and I were old enough to go quite a ways from home and run between houses in a merry chase to get more candy. At the end of the night we poured out our stash onto the floor and sorted it. Always we gave a favorite piece to our mother and father. Then the trading began, "I don't like this one but I do like that. Will you trade two of this one for one of that?" Finally we were satisfied with our trades and begin to count the candies. Those were golden years. I had more than 365 pieces and I could have a piece of candy every day for an entire year. I would stash my treasure in my drawer and each day take out a sweet treasure after school to enjoy, my reward for the day.

Assignment

Your assignment today includes writing a very short poem. Western poetry often has a special rhythm to it. If a person claps the words when the poem is read the rhythm soon emerges with louder and softer claps. It also contains rhyming words, words that have the same ending sound.

Take note the poem "Trees" by -- Joyce Kilmer. Each set of two lines ends in a word that rhymes with the other line. The ear hears this natural melody and expects it. The rhyming gives the poem an auditory beauty as the mind makes a picture.

Trees

I THINK that I shall never see
A poem lovely as a tree.
A tree whose hungry mouth is prest (pressed)
Against the sweet earth's flowing breast;

A tree that looks at God all day, 5
And lifts her leafy arms to pray;
A tree that may in summer wear
A nest of robins in her hair;
Upon whose bosom snow has lain;
Who intimately lives with rain. 9
Poems are made by fools like me,
But only God can make a tree.

Each line of the poem has 4 beats to it, "I **think** that **I** shall **nev**er **see** a **poem** as **lov**ely **as** a **tree**." This makes the poem almost a song with a beautiful swinging rhythm. Read it out loud and listen for the natural rhythm it has.

Note the poet takes what is called poetic license. He breaks a rule to make something work in his poem. He takes pressed and changes it to "prest" to make it rhyme with "breast".

This lovely poem is crafted to reach us on multiple levels. Our ears hear the melody, our eyes make a picture and our sensory system resonates with the meaning of the poem. The reader may even remember the smell of a favorite tree or a forest and find all of these sensory intakes come together for a wonderful synesthesia.

Now it is your turn to write a short poem. Before you start go to the assignment worksheet. Start the assignment by writing rhyming words. This will give you a start on words you can end your lines with. Then start on the poem. Craft it so the lines rhyme and the poem has a natural rhythm to it. Your poem needs only be four to eight lines long. Write about Halloween, autumn or another subject your teacher assigns or suggests. Maybe you will "be a poet, but didn't know it."

Sample Poems

The poems below are popular poems with children in the United States. They are often done as songs and finger plays.

HALLOWEEN POEMS

Pumpkins and the Witch
Five little pumpkins sitting on a fence
A witch came riding by.
Ho, ho, ho I'll take you all
And make you a pumpkin pie.

When it's Halloween
When it's Halloween!
Monsters can be seen,
Hiding here,
Hiding there,
Hiding all to scare, ---Boo!

Five Little Pumpkins
Five little pumpkins sitting on a gate,
The first one said, "Oh, my, it's getting late."
The second one said, "There are witches in the air."
The third one said, "But we don't care."
The fourth one said, "Let's run and run and run."
The fifth one said, "I'm ready for some fun!"
Oh, hhhh went the wind and out went the light,
And the five little pumpkins rolled out of sight.

Black and Gold
Everything is black and gold, black and gold to night.
Yellow pumpkin, yellow moon, yellow candlelight.

Jet black cat with golden eyes. Shadows black as ink.
Firelight twinkling in the dark, with a yellow blink.

Black and gold, black and gold. Nothing in between.
When the world is black and gold, then it's Halloween.
---Nancy Byrd Turner (1880-1971)

Lesson 10: Poetry

Homework Assignment

- Choose a poem from the ones in the reading assignment.
- Discuss the meaning of the poem.
- Relate it to your life and experiences in some way.
- This is to be your own thoughts, not copied of the internet. No Plagiarism!
- Thoughts should be 100-300 words.
- Include the poem (cut it out or highlight and paste is ok).
- Only use a poem for the list given in the reading assignment.

Weekly Reading

Poetry
Choose one of these poems and discuss what it means to you.

Tangerine
When once I leave this body
Shall I not come back to the world?
If only I might return
Upon a winter's evening
Taking on the compassionate flesh of a cold tangerine
At the bedside of some dying acquaintance.
(tr. unknown)

Portrait of a Raspberry
Just as raspberry runners travel under the sand
and put out new shoots each year
he had travelled
far from his beginnings, had forgotten
and since he only lived in his outpost,
his remotest rootlet, thought he was new
and singular to the species.
If he'd turned round
he'd have seen similar bushes the whole way:
even in the mother-bush the one he was.
(tr. Anne Born)

Cherries
Cherries, cherries, ruby red,
want to try one? Go ahead!
Cherry pie or cherries jubilee,
find the pit and plant a cherry tree.

They'll stain your mouth and hands bright red,
so never eat cherries under the covers in bed.

~ Nursery Rhyme

To my wife

You bring coolness to the halls
A sense of space to rooms
To wake in your bed in the morning
Gives me daylong joy

We are two halves of the same apple
Our day and night
Our house and home are one
Happiness is a meadow
Where you tread
It springs to life
Loneliness comes from the road you go down

(tr. Ruth Christie & Richard McKane)

Grapes

Luscious grapes grow by the bunch.
Grapes are easy to pack for lunch.
In an arbor, on a vine,
Red or green, they taste just fine.
Some have seeds, but others don't.
Turn down a grape? I know I won't!
You know what I think is most fun?
Just sit and eat them, one by one.
(tr. unknown)

Fruit Poem: A Lover

The plums and cherries are blossoming,
My heart too is unsheathing from winter —
And it has all happened in one day.
By Witter Bynner

Sample Poetries

My Cherry Rewards

I love cherries. I have a fruit orchard in my home in Idaho where we have two cherry trees. One is a pie cherry tree. Often people will turn up their noses and walk away from pie cherries as they are small and have a large stone or pit in the middle with little fruit surrounding it. But I know the goodness of the little tart balls for I am the picker and I climb the tree. As I reach for the small fruit, the sweet juice trickles down my arms and soon I am a sweet, sticky, cherry mess with a mouth full of tart, ripe berries as an immediate reward for all the work I am putting in and a dream of cherry turnovers hot from the oven. Only one who picks the fruit can know the full rewards of the pie cherry and I am one of those. Care to join me?

By Debrah Roundy 157 words

Reading on Using Articles

This information may be on your next Fix It.

What is an article? It is an adjective that modifies a noun. In English there are three words used as articles: the, a, and an. "The" is called a definite article because it refers to something definite or specific. For instance, <u>the cat</u> refers to a specific cat, not just any cat. "A" or "an" are indefinite articles because they do not refer to something definite. For example, <u>a cat</u> could be any cat.

How do you know which one to use, "a" or "an"?

- a + singular noun beginning with a consonant: *a car; a truck; a van; a cycle; a scooter*
- an + singular noun beginning with a vowel: *an elephant; an ostrich; an anteater; an ant*
- a + singular noun beginning with a consonant sound: *a user* (sounds like 'yoo-zer.' It. begins with a consonant 'y' sound, so 'a' is used); *a unicorn*; *a university*
- an + nouns starting with silent "h": *an hour*
- an + acronyms with a vowel sound even though it is a consonant: an MBA
- a + acronyms that have a consonant sound a Ph.D., a B.A.,

Count and Non count Nouns

The can be used with none count nouns, or the article can be omitted entirely.

- "I love to swim in the water" (some specific body of water) or "I love to swim in water" (any water).
- "He spilled the juice all over the floor" (some specific drink, perhaps the juice he had at the party) or "He spilled juice all over the floor" (any milk).

"A/an" can be used only with count nouns.

- "I need a bottle of water."
- "I need a new glass of juice."

Most of the time, you can't say, "She wants a water," unless you're implying, say, a bottle of water.

Geographical nouns also have some rules.

Do not use “the” before:

- names of most countries/territories: *China, Malaysia, Japan*
- however use the with these countries: *the* Netherlands, *the* Dominican Republic, *the* Philippines, *the* United States
- names of cities, towns, or states: *Shanghai, Seoul, Hong Kong, Kobe*
- names of streets: *Huashan Road, , Main St.*
- names of lakes and bays: *Lake Baikal, Lake Erie*
- except with a group of lakes like *the Great Lakes*
- names of mountains: *Mount Everest, Mount Fuji*
- except with ranges of mountains like *the Andes* or *the Sierra Nevada's*
- or unusual names like *the Matterhorn*
- names of continents: Asia, Africa, South America
- names of islands (Honolulu, Maui, Key West)
- except with island chains like the Aleutians, the Hawaiian Islands, or the Canary Islands

Do use the before:

- names of rivers, oceans and seas: *the Snake , the Pacific*
- points on the globe: *the Equator, the South Pole*
- geographical areas: *the Mediterranean, the South*
- deserts, forests, gulfs, and peninsulas: *the Gobi, the Gulf of Mexico, the Caribou Forest, the Iberian Peninsula*

Some common types of nouns that don't take an article are:

- Names of languages and nationalities: *Chinese, Japanese, Spanish, Korean* (unless you are referring to the population of the nation: "**The** Fujian’s are known for their warm hospitality.")
- Names of sports: *football, soccer, tai chi*
- Names of academic subjects: *English, mathematics, biology, physical education*

Lesson 11: Writing a Pro/Con Essay

Homework Assignment

- One Child Policy (or other as assigned by the teacher).
- Create a LLA chart to base your essay from.
- Write one paragraph with a brief explanation of the issue you are writing about.
- Write one paragraph pro (for) the issue.
- Write one paragraph con (or against) the issue.
- In this assignment it is not necessary to write which way you think but many students want to share that and you may share your opinion of the issue in a final paragraph.

Weekly Reading

Take a look at the One-child Policy of China or another article that your teacher gives you that has two sides. You can discuss it from today's perspective or a perspective when it was fully enforced in the past. Start by first gathering your ideas. Look at it from both sides. There is a famous presupposition in NLP that says, "Every action has a positive intention." This means that everyone and everything has a positive reason behind it. If you only argue from your side you will miss the positive intention of the other side. Understanding both sides gives your essay strength. This essay will explore looking at an issue from both sides.

Write a paragraph supporting your reason, and then write another paragraph rejecting your reason. Look at the issue from both sides.

Do not use quotes and famous sayings. You may use personal experiences. This assignment is to be your thoughts not the thoughts of great sages. Maybe one day you will be a great sage, who knows? However you can research the topic and use their thinking to help you formulate your ideas and arguments. It is fine to use statistics and if you do, make sure you recognize that at the bottom of your paper. Put enough information down that the reader could look it up if interested. Later in the year we will learn to write source citations. If you already know how to do that, you may do that is this essay.

It is normally acceptable to use quotes and sayings in essays, but in this class you are here for a specific reason, to help you with your English writing. When you are quoting someone there is nothing for the teacher to correct. Quotes and sayings enhance essays showing you have researched and are able to cognitively put together new learning with previous learning. Here you are to focus on another issue, helping you be the best and most creative English writer you can be. Please do not use many quotes in your writing unless they are really needed.

Neurolinguists learn a pattern called Logical Level Alignment. It comes from the work of Gregory Bateson. There are natural hierarchies of classification. Each level organizes the information on the level below. We will use this LLA format for your essay. These are the levels of the LLA. Notice that we start at the bottom with the environment and move up the levels to the purpose which is the pinnacle or peak of the issue. As you work through this LLA you will find that I helps you organize your ideas and arguments effectively. You can use these to very effectively write your essay. You will find that your essay will flow into form for you.

Let's take a look at it.

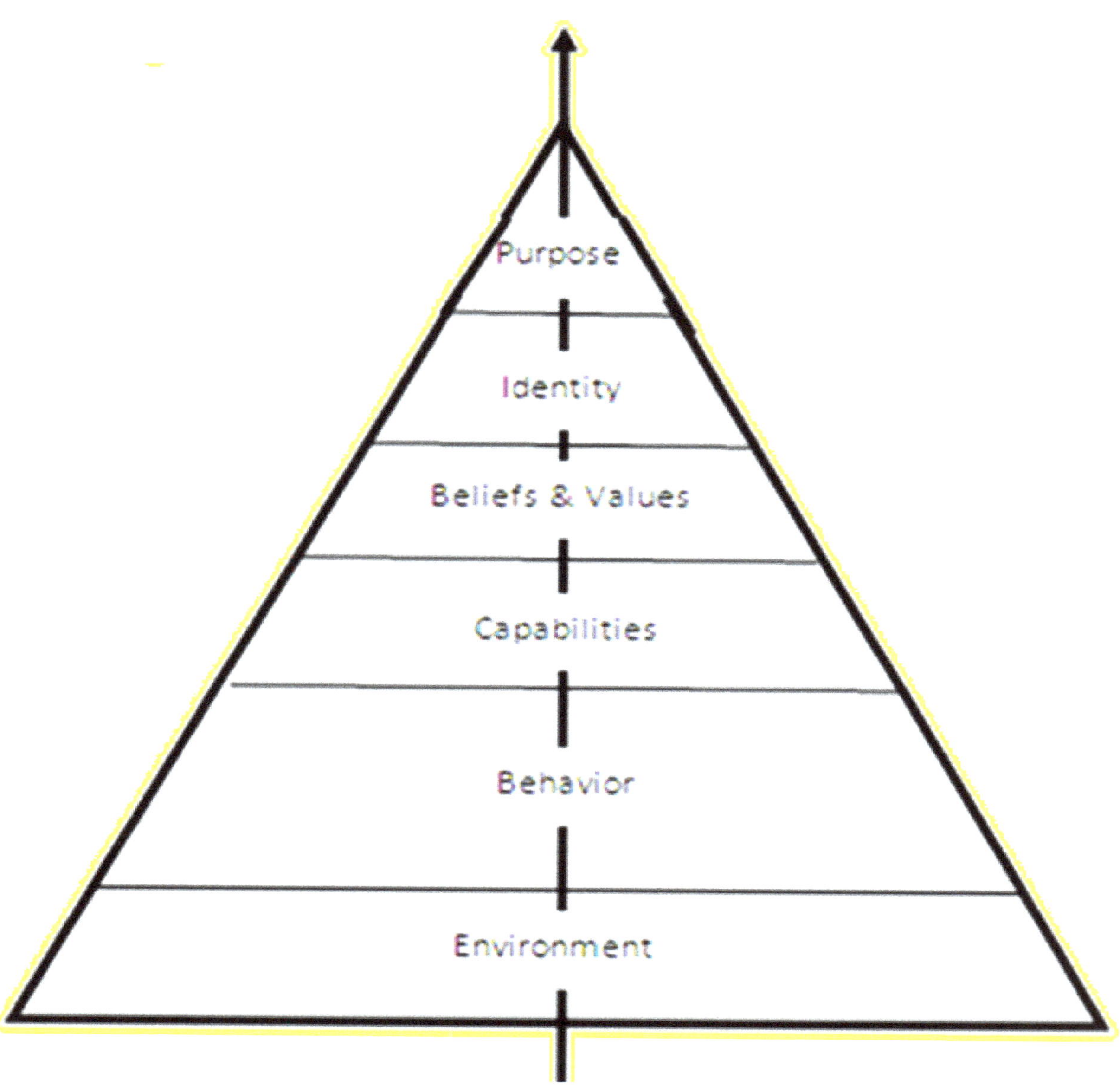

Here is an explanation of those levels

	answers
Environment	Answers the questions when and where
Behavior	Answers ***What?*** The actions and reactions to the environment
Capability	Answers ***How? What*** strategies are used?
Beliefs and values	Answers ***why*** we do the things we do?
	the values and meanings a person or organization puts on things in life
Identity	Answers **Who** am I ?
Purpose	Answers the questions "For Whom" or "For what?" Purpose reaches beyond our body and into the greater field of time and space.

Choose one side. Look at it from the neurological levels. Write your paragraph. Then take the other side and do the same thing. Here is an example using the issue of eating organic foods as a topic.

Eating Organic Foods		
	pro	con
Environment	home	home
Behavior	choose organic food for my family as a first choice every time	choose inexpensive food as a first choice
Capability	Choosing organic foods that are healthy making healthy choices for my family	choosing foods that my family can afford watching the budget and getting the best value for my money
Beliefs and values	believe that organic foods will give bodies great strength and energy to grow	believe that all food is healthy and that getting the best value for the money is important
	value organic choices	value having enough food to feed the family and getting a good value
Identity	I am a person who values healthy eating even if it costs more.	I am a person who can provide enough food for my family while keeping within the family budget.
Purpose	My family will be healthy through my work	My family will be healthy through my work

Next is an article on the one child policy. There are many more on the internet to help you out. Remember if you quote from an article, to put the quote in quotation marks and tell the reader who said it.

Chinese think tank urges end to one-child policy

By ALEXA OLESEN | Associated Press – *15 hrs ago*

BEIJING (AP) — A Chinese government think tank is urging the country's leaders to start phasing out its one-child policy immediately and allow two children for every family by 2015, a daring proposal to do away with the unpopular policy.

Some demographers see the timeline put forward by the China Development Research Foundation as a bold move by the body close to the central leadership. Others warn that the gradual approach, if implemented, would still be insufficient to help correct the problems that China's strict birth limits have created.

XieMeng, a press affairs official with the foundation, said the final version of the report wil be released "in a week or two." But Chinese state media have been given advance copies. The official Xinhua News Agency said the foundation recommends a two-child policy in some provinces from this year and a nationwide two-child policy by 2015. It proposes all birth limits be dropped by 2020, Xinhua reported.

"China has paid a huge political and social cost for the policy, as it has resulted in social conflict, high administrative costs and led indirectly to a long-term gender imbalance at birth," Xinhua said, citing the report.

But it remains unclear whether Chinese leaders are ready to take up the recommendations. China's National Population and Family Planning Commission had no immediate comment on the report Wednesday.

Known to many as the one-child policy, China's actual rules are more complicated. The government limits most urban couples to one child, and allows two children for rural families if their first-born is a girl. There are numerous other exceptions as well, including looser rules for minority families and a two-child limit for parents who are themselves both singletons.

Cai Yong, an assistant professor of sociology at the University of North Carolina, Chapel Hill, said the report holds extra weight because the think tank is under the State Council, China's Cabinet. He said he found it remarkable that state-backed demographers were willing to publicly propose such a detailed schedule and plan on how to get rid of China's birth limits.

"That tells us at least that policy change is inevitable, it's coming," said Cai, who was not involved in the drafting of the report but knows many of the experts who were. Cai is currently a visiting scholar at Fudan University in Shanghai. "It's coming, but we cannot predict when exactly it will come."

Adding to the uncertainty is a once-in-a-decade leadership transition that kicks off Nov. 8 (2012) that will see a new slate of top leaders installed by next spring. Cai said the transition could keep population reform on the back burner or changes might be rushed through to help burnish the reputations of President Hu Jintao and Premier Wen Jiabao on their way out.

There has been growing speculation among Chinese media, experts and ordinary people about whether the government will soon relax the one-child policy — introduced in 1980 as a temporary measure to curb surging population growth — and allow more people to have two children.

Though the government credits the policy with preventing hundreds of millions of births and helping lift countless families out of poverty, it is reviled by many ordinary people. The strict limits have led to forced abortions and sterilizations, even though such measures are illegal. Couples who flout the rules face hefty fines, seizure of their property and loss of their jobs.

Many demographers argue that the policy has worsened the country's aging crisis by limiting the size of the young labor pool that must support the large baby boom generation as it retires. They say it has contributed to the imbalanced sex ratio by encouraging families to abort baby girls, preferring to try for a male heir.

The government recognizes those problems and has tried to address them by boosting social services for the elderly. It has also banned sex-selective abortion and rewarded rural families whose only child is a girl.

Many today also see the birth limits as outdated, a relic of the era when housing, jobs and food were provided by the state.

"It has been thirty years since our planned economy was liberalized," commented Wang Yi, the owner of a shop that sells textiles online, under a news report on the foundation's proposal. "So why do we still have to plan our population?"

Though open debate about the policy has flourished in state media and on the Internet, leaders have so far expressed a desire to maintain the status quo. President Hu said last year that China would keep its strict family planning policy to keep the birth rate low and other officials have said that no changes are expected until at least 2015.

Wang Feng, director of the Brookings-Tsinghua Center for Public Policy and an expert on China's demographics, contributed research material to the foundation's report but has yet to see the full text. He said he welcomed the gist of the document that he's seen in state media.

It says the government "should return the rights of reproduction to the people," he said. "That's very bold."

GuBaochang, a professor of demography at Beijing's Renmin University and a vocal advocate of reform, said the proposed timeline wasn't aggressive enough. should have reformed this policy ages ago," he said. "It just keeps getting held up, delayed."

Associated Press researcher Flora Ji in Beijing contributed to this report.

Sample Essay

Name
Student Number
Assignment 11
Essay word count 354

Eating Organic Foods		
	Pro	Con
Environment	usually grown locally	often grown all over the world so there is more variety
Behavior	choose organic food for my family as a first choice every time	choose inexpensive food as a first choice
Capability	Choosing organic foods that are healthy making healthy choices for my family	choosing foods that my family can afford watching the budget and getting the best value for my money
Beliefs and values	believe that organic foods will give bodies great strength and energy to grow	believe that all food is healthy and that getting the best value for the money is important
	value organic choices	value having enough food to feed the family, good variety and getting a good value
Identity	I am a person who values healthy eating even if it costs more.	I am a person who can provide enough food for my family while keeping within the family budget.
Purpose	My family will be healthy through my work	My family will be healthy through my work

Pros and Cons of Eating Organic Foods

There is a lot of controversy about the types of food we eat. One controversy is over organic vs. inorganic foods. What is the difference? Organic food is generally grown without the use of chemical fertilizers or herbicides. Because of this it is often more labor intensive to raise organic foods and they often cost more in the market place. Non organic foods are foods that may have chemicals including herbicides and pesticide applied to them or to the ground they are grown on. They may also be genetically modified. Some people think that organic food is tastier but others like the plain and milder taste of nonorganic food.

Organic food proponents like food grown closer to home because they feel it is a healthier choice for their bodies and for their families. They believe that organic foods will give them more energy and strength. Often proponents of organic food choices are people who strongly identify with healthy eating habits and are willing to pay more for their food because they truly believe that their family will be healthier.

On the other hand there are people who choose nonorganic choices. They like the variety of food available grown all over the world that is often a lower cost option and believe it gives them the widest choice for the best value and keeps the family budget in balance. Proponents of nonorganic food choices identify with being able to provide that food while keeping in the family budget and value a healthy family through their work at purchasing a wide variety of foods available in the market place.

As for me, I purchase both organic and nonorganic fruits and vegetables. I like to support the local farmers and have the fuller flavor that comes with organic produce. I even raise an organic garden of my own and feast from it all year round. I also like to add to my diet the many food choices that are available from all over the world and not limit myself to the narrow range of produce that is locally grown. By eating both I am able to have a rich and varied diet at a price that I can afford.

Meta Model Presupposition

In this lesson a new Meta Model pattern is introduced, presupposition: X is assumed true so Y is also presupposed to be true. Vicky is beautiful so she is popular with the guys. (X - Vicky is beautiful) so (Y - she is popular with the guys.) must be true. Vicky may be popular because she is beautiful however it could also be that she has a warm and friendly personality. It is also possible that even though she is beautiful, she really is not popular with the guys because they find her intimidating.

With presuppositions we clarify our stand of why X = Y. Here are some questions that may challenge the presupposition:

Is Vicky beautiful? Who says or by what standard are you judging her beauty?
Are there guys who are intimidated by beautiful girls?
How do you know she is popular with the guys, what are the evidences?

Here is an example of a sentence clarifying the presupposition. Notice how it addresses both her beauty and her popularity making both her beauty and her popularity clear with facts to back it up.

Vicky, whom all the girls and guys in our class voted most beautiful, is also popular with the guys because she smiles at them and takes the time to chat with them in the halls at school so she always has a small gathering of boys around her.

Watch for the Meta Model pattern presupposition in your classwork in the next week or two.

Lesson 12: Copyright Ways and Haiku

Homework Assignment

Read the article on copyright violations and write one paragraph about how you feel about copyrights.

Next week our lesson will be on thankfulness. Read about Haiku Poetry and write one Haiku about something you are thankful for. Your teacher will be looking for the 5-7-5 syllable Haiku pattern in your poem.

Weekly Reading

Read the article about copyrights, and then write one paragraph about your current view of copyrights. Answer one question in your article. If you were a writer who made your living from your work, how would you feel if others used your work without permission?

China slams "distorted" view of copyright piracy problem

By Ben Blanchard

BEIJING (Reuters) - China's top official in charge of fighting copyright piracy on Sunday slammed what he said was deliberate distortion of the problem by the Western media caused by the country's poor global image, saying important facts had been ignored.

Foreign governments, including the United States, have for years urged China to take a stronger stand against pervasive violations of intellectual property rights on products ranging from medicines to software to DVD movies sold on the street.

The United States in April again put China, along with Russia, on its annual list of countries with the worst records of preventing the theft of copyrighted material and other intellectual property.

But Tian Lipu, head of China's State Intellectual Property Office, said the government's efforts were being ignored.

"Speaking honestly, there is a market. People use and buy pirated goods," Tian told reporters on the sidelines of a landmark Communist Party congress.

"To a large extent, China's intellectual property rights protection image has been distorted by Western media.

"China's image overseas is very poor. As soon as people hear China they think or piracy and counterfeiting -- (Beijing's) Sanlitun, that place in Shanghai, Luohu in Shenzhen," he said, referring to places notorious for selling fake goods.

"We don't deny (this problem), and we are continuing to battle against it," Tian added.

But other facts were overlooked, he said.

"For example, China is the world's largest payer for patent rights, for trademark rights, for royalties, and one of the largest for buying real software," he said. "We pay the most. People rarely talk about this, but it really is a fact. Our government offices, our banks, our insurance companies, our firms ... the software is all real."

Microsoft Corp and other members of the Business Software Alliance in the United States complain that nearly 80 percent of the software installed on personal computers in China is pirated.

Tian said that if companies like Apple Inc. were so worried by piracy they would never choose China for their production bases.

"Of the goods made for Apple, most are made in China. Once Apple's brand is added to it and it is exported to the United States its value doubles," he said.

"This could only happen because China's intellectual property rights environment sets foreign investors at ease allowing them to come to China to manufacture."

The International Intellectual Property Alliance, a U.S. coalition of film, software, music and publishing groups, estimates that U.S. companies lost more than $15 billion in 2009 due to international copyright theft.

About $14 billion of the total was due to software piracy, with an estimated $3.5 billion in losses in China and $1.4 billion in Russia.

Blanchard, Ben. (Editing by Ron Popeski). *China slams "distorted" View of Copyright Piracy Problem. Web. November 11, 2012.* <http://www.reuters.com/article/2012/11/11/us-china-congress-piracy-idUSBRE8AA04620121111>

Next week we will learn about a Canadian and United States Holiday called Thanksgiving. People in America often share with others the things and people they are grateful for in their lives. It is an autumn holiday where the entire family gets together to celebrate. There is a lot of feasting and wonderful meals. At the meals people share the blessings they are thankful for that year.

About Haiku

What is a Haiku poem? It is a Japanese poetry form loved in the USA. Read below for more information. Write a Haiku Poem on something you are grateful for.

Haiku is a poetry form based on rhythm, not rhyme. Traditional haiku consists of 17 “mora” or units. These 17 units are in three phrases of 5 mora , seven mora and five mora, the 5-7-5 pattern.

In Japanese haiku a cutting word called a kiriji, appears at the end of one of the verse's three phrases. Although it can be at the end of any of the phrases it typically is at the end of the poem providing a strong and dignified ending as well as a sense of closure to the poem.

A favorite poet in Japan is the 17th century poet Bashō. He traveled around Japan writing and sharing his poetry with others. People today still follow his path traveling Japan and looking for beauty to share in their own poetry. Here is one of his poems.

the first cold show'r
ev'n the monkey seems to want
a small coat of straw

Note there is some poetic license in the translation as two words are shortened into single syllables to produce the 5-7-5 on pattern.

Here is another. Again notice the 5-7-5 pattern.

An old silent pond...
A frog jumps into the pond,
splash! Silence again.

Example

Teaching in China

Wonderful students, such fun

I'm glad I came, love!

Meta Model

In the next lesson you may encounter the Meta Model pattern called **Mind Reading or The Crystal Ball.** A crystal ball is a clear ball made of quartz crystal fortunetellers look into to see the future. The pattern presupposes you assume that you know something that you do not really know. The challenge is to ask how the writer knows and the answer is to clarify who the writer knows.

Example: (I know you aren't happy)

Challenge: How do you know I am not happy?
Do you have a crystal ball?
Can you read my mind?

Answer: I see you are frowning and looking worried, are you unhappy?
You are so quiet today, are you unhappy about something?

I know there will be a Chrystal Ball in your classwork next week if your teacher follows the syllabus.

Sample Use of Copyrighted Material

Some of the information used on copyrights was obtained from a friend, Robert Dilts, who is an author. I asked to use this information and here is the permission granted:

Sure Deb.
That would be fine.
It is important to get accurate and clear information out regarding intellectual property rights.
With gratitude,
Robert

Lesson 13: Thanksgiving and a Christmas Carol

Homework Assignment

Quiz Stave 1

1. Scrooge was Marley's his sole friend. How many friends did Marley have?
2. How does the knocker change?
3. What has Marley's ghost been doing since his death?
4. What is the warning that Marley gives Scrooge?
5. What is Marley's first name?

Weekly Reading

The Thanksgiving Story

Most stories of Thanksgiving start with the harvest celebration of the pilgrims and the Native Americans that took place in the autumn of 1621. They did have a three-day feast in celebration of a good harvest, and the local Native Americans did participate, however this "First Thanksgiving" was not a holiday, only a gathering of celebration. Still it was remembered as a time of celebration and the story was passed from mother to child over the ensuing years. Thanksgiving as an official holiday can, however, be traced back to 1863 when Pres. Lincoln became the first president to proclaim Thanksgiving Day. The holiday has been a fixture of late November ever since.

However, since most school children are taught that the first Thanksgiving was held in 1621 with the pilgrims and Native Americans, let us take a closer look at just what took place leading up to that event, and then what happened in the centuries afterward that finally gave us our modern Thanksgiving.

The Pilgrims who sailed to this country aboard the very small ship called the *Mayflower* were members of the English Separatist Church, a part of the Puritan sect. Some years earlier they had fled their homes in England and sailed to Holland (The Netherlands) to escape religious persecution. There, they enjoyed more religious tolerance, but they eventually became disenchanted with the Dutch way of life, thinking it ungodly. Seeking a better life, the Separatists negotiated with a London stock company to finance a pilgrimage to America. Most of those making the trip aboard the Mayflower were not a part of the religious group of Pilgrims but were hired to protect the company's interests. Only about one-third of the original colonists were Separatists.

The Pilgrims looked at several locations before choosing to set ground at Plymouth Rock on December 11, 1620. Their first winter was devastating. In the ten months that followed, the group had lost forty-six of the original one hundred and two people who sailed on the *Mayflower*. Fortunately, the harvest of 1621 was a bountiful one. The remaining colonists decided to celebrate with a feast and invited a few of their neighboring Indians. Imagine their surprise when ninety-one Native Americans showed up. It is believed that the Pilgrims would not have made it through the year without the help of the natives who showed them what natural and native plants and animals they could eat, showed them how to plant crops and how to hunt in a very different and wild land than they had left. The feast was more of a traditional English harvest festival than a true "thanksgiving" observance. It lasted three days.

Governor William Bradford sent "four men fowling" after wild ducks and geese. It is not certain that wild turkey was part of their feast, however, it is certain that they had venison. The term "turkey" was used by the Pilgrims to mean any sort of wild fowl.

At almost every modern Thanksgiving table is pumpkin pie. But it is unlikely that the first feast included that treat. The supply of flour was nearly gone, so there was no bread or pastries of any kind. We know that they did eat boiled pumpkin, and they produced a type of fried bread from their corn crop. There was also no milk, cider, potatoes, or butter. There was no domestic cattle for dairy products, and the newly-discovered potato was still considered by many Europeans to be poisonous. But the feast did include fish, berries, watercress, lobster, dried fruit, clams, venison, and plums.

This Thanksgiving feast was not repeated the following year. Many years passed before the event was repeated. It wasn't until June of 1676 that another Day of Thanksgiving was proclaimed. On June 20 of that year the governing council of Charlestown, Massachusetts, held a meeting to determine how best to express thanks for the good fortune that had seen their community securely established. By unanimous vote they instructed Edward Rawson, the clerk, to proclaim June 29 as a Day of Thanksgiving. This thanksgiving celebration probably did not include the Native Americans, as the celebration was meant partly to be in recognition of the colonists' recent victory over the "heathen natives. Your author, Debrah Roundy, is a descendent of Edward Rawson and of William Bradford making Thanksgiving day an especially important family celebration.

The next known celebration was one hundred years later, in October of 1777. At that time all Thirteen Colonies joined in a thanksgiving celebration to commemorate the patriotic victory over the British at Saratoga. It was a one-time affair. Just a few years later George Washington proclaimed a National Day of Thanksgiving in 1789, although some were opposed to it. There was disharmony among the colonies, many feeling the hardships of a few pilgrims did not warrant a national holiday. Later, President Thomas Jefferson opposed the idea of having a day of thanksgiving.

It was a woman, Sarah Josepha Hale, a magazine editor, whose efforts eventually led to what we recognize as Thanksgiving. Hale wrote many editorials championing her cause in her *Boston Ladies' Magazine,* and later, in *Godey's Lady's Book.* Finally, after a 40-year campaign of writing editorials and letters to governors and presidents, Hale's dedication became a reality when, in 1863, President Lincoln proclaimed the *last* Thursday in November as a national day of Thanksgiving. Thanksgiving has been proclaimed by every president after Lincoln and in 1941, Thanksgiving was finally sanctioned by Congress as a legal holiday, as the *fourth* Thursday in November.

This week you are to read Stave 1 of a Christmas Carol. This book was written in 1843 by Charles Dickens. He was saddened by the lot of poor children and indeed spent time as a youth poor, having to sell all of his books and work in a factory when bad times fell on his family. This book is written in 5 chapters called Staves at that time. We will do one each week. Enjoy the story as you get glimpses of old England in the 18th century, a time of industrial revolution and change.

A CHRISTMAS CAROL

By Charles Dickens

Stave 1: *Marley's Ghost*

Marley was dead: to begin with. There is no doubt whatever about that. The register of his burial was signed by the clergyman, the clerk, the undertaker, and the chief mourner. Scrooge signed it: and Scrooge's name was good upon 'Change, for anything he chose to put his hand to. Old Marley was as dead as a door-nail.

Mind! I don't mean to say that I know, of my own knowledge, what there is particularly dead about a door-nail. I might have been inclined, myself, to regard a coffin-nail as the deadest piece of ironmongery in the trade. But the wisdom of our ancestors is in the simile; and my unhallowed hands shall not disturb it, or the Country's done for. You will therefore permit me to repeat, emphatically, that Marley was as dead as a door-nail.

Scrooge knew he was dead? Of course he did. How could it be otherwise? Scrooge and he were partners for I don't know how many years. Scrooge was his sole executor, his sole administrator, his sole assign, his sole residuary legatee, his sole friend and sole mourner. And even Scrooge was not so dreadfully cut up by the sad event, but that he was an excellent man of business on the very day of the funeral, and solemnised it with an undoubted bargain.

The mention of Marley's funeral brings me back to the point I started from. There is no doubt that Marley was dead. This must be distinctly understood, or nothing wonderful can come of the story I am going to relate. If we were not perfectly convinced that Hamlet's Father died before the play began, there would be nothing more remarkable in his taking a stroll at night, in an easterly wind, upon his own ramparts, than there would be in any other middle-aged gentleman rashly turning out after dark in a breezy spot -- say Saint Paul's Churchyard for instance -- literally to astonish his son's weak mind.

Scrooge never painted out Old Marley's name. There it stood, years afterwards, above the warehouse door: Scrooge and Marley. The firm was known as Scrooge and Marley. Sometimes people new to the business called Scrooge Scrooge, and sometimes Marley, but he answered to both names: it was all the same to him.

Oh! But he was a tight-fisted hand at the grind- stone, Scrooge! a squeezing, wrenching, grasping, scraping, clutching, covetous, old sinner! Hard and sharp as flint, from which no steel had ever struck out generous fire; secret, and self-contained, and solitary as an oyster. The cold within him froze his old features, nipped his pointed nose, shriveled his cheek, stiffened his gait; made his eyes red, his thin lips blue and spoke out shrewdly in his grating voice. A frosty rime was on his head, and on his eyebrows, and his wiry chin. He carried his own low temperature always about with him; he iced his office in the dogdays; and didn't thaw it one degree at Christmas.

External heat and cold had little influence on Scrooge. No warmth could warm, no wintry weather chill him. No wind that blew was bitterer than he; no falling snow was more intent upon its purpose, no pelting rain less open to entreaty. Foul weather didn't know where to have him. The heaviest rain, and snow, and hail, and sleet, could boast of the advantage over him in only one respect. They often "came down" handsomely, and Scrooge never did.

Nobody ever stopped him in the street to say, with gladsome looks, "My dear Scrooge, how are you? When will you come to see me?" No beggars implored him to bestow a trifle, no children asked him what it was o'clock, no man or woman ever once in all his life inquired the way to such and such a place, of Scrooge. Even the blind men's dogs appeared to know him; and when they saw him coming on, would tug their owners into doorways and up courts; and then would wag their tails as though they said, "No eye at all is better than an evil eye, dark master!"

But what did Scrooge care? It was the very thing he liked. To edge his way along the crowded paths of life, warning all human sympathy to keep its distance, was what the knowing ones call "nuts" to Scrooge.

Once upon a time -- of all the good days in the year, on Christmas Eve -- old Scrooge sat busy in his counting-house. It was cold, bleak, biting weather: foggy withal: and he could hear the people in the court outside go wheezing up and down, beating their hands upon their breasts, and stamping their feet upon the pavement stones to warm them. The city clocks had only just gone three, but it was quite dark already -- it had not been light all day: and candles were flaring in the windows of the neighbouring offices, like ruddy smears upon the palpable brown air. The fog came pouring in at every chink and keyhole, and was so dense without, that although the court was of the narrowest, the houses opposite were mere phantoms. To see the dingy cloud come drooping down, obscuring everything, one might have thought that Nature lived hard by, and was brewing on a large scale.

The door of Scrooge's counting-house was open that he might keep his eye upon his clerk, who in a dismal little cell beyond, a sort of tank, was copying letters. Scrooge had a very small fire, but the clerk's fire was so very much smaller that it looked like one coal. But he couldn't replenish it, for Scrooge kept the coal-box in his own room; and so surely as the clerk came in with the shovel, the master predicted that it would be necessary for them to part. Wherefore the clerk put on his white comforter, and tried to warm himself at the candle; in which effort, not being a man of a strong imagination, he failed.

"A merry Christmas, uncle! God save you!" cried a cheerful voice. It was the voice of Scrooge's nephew, who came upon him so quickly that this was the first intimation he had of his approach.

"Bah!" said Scrooge, "Humbug!"

He had so heated himself with rapid walking in the fog and frost, this nephew of Scrooge's, that he was all in a glow; his face was ruddy and handsome; his eyes sparkled, and his breath smoked again.

"Christmas a humbug, uncle!" said Scrooge's nephew. "You don't mean that, I am sure."

"I do," said Scrooge. "Merry Christmas! What right have you to be merry? What reason have you to be merry? You're poor enough."

"Come, then," returned the nephew gaily. "What right have you to be dismal? What reason have you to be morose? You're rich enough."

Scrooge having no better answer ready on the spur of the moment, said "Bah!" again; and followed it up with "Humbug."

"Don't be cross, uncle!" said the nephew.

"What else can I be," returned the uncle, "when I live in such a world of fools as this? Merry Christmas! Out upon merry Christmas! What's Christmas time to you but a time for paying bills without money; a time for finding yourself a year older, but not an hour richer; a time for balancing your books and having every item in 'em through a round dozen of months presented dead against you? If I could work my will," said Scrooge indignantly, "every idiot who goes about with 'Merry Christmas' on his lips, should be boiled with his own pudding, and buried with a stake of holly through his heart. He should!"

"Uncle!" pleaded the nephew.

"Nephew!" returned the uncle, sternly, "keep Christmas in your own way, and let me keep it in mine."

"Keep it!" repeated Scrooge's nephew. "But you don't keep it."

"Let me leave it alone, then," said Scrooge. "Much good may it do you! Much good it has ever done you!"

"There are many things from which I might have derived good, by which I have not profited, I dare say," returned the nephew. "Christmas among the rest. But I am sure I have always thought of Christmas time, when it has come round -- apart from the veneration due to its sacred name and origin, if anything belonging to it can be apart from that -- as a good time: a kind, forgiving, charitable, pleasant time: the only time I know of, in the long calendar of the year, when men and women seem by one consent to open their shut-up hearts freely, and to think of people below them as if they really were fellow-passengers to the grave, and not another race of creatures bound on other journeys. And therefore, uncle, though it has never put a scrap of gold or silver in my pocket, I believe that it *has* done me good, and *will* do me good; and I say, God bless it!"

The clerk in the tank involuntarily applauded: becoming immediately sensible of the impropriety, he poked the fire, and extinguished the last frail spark for ever.

"Let me hear another sound from *you*," said Scrooge, "and you'll keep your Christmas by losing your situation. You're quite a powerful speaker, sir," he added, turning to his nephew. "I wonder you don't go into Parliament."

"Don't be angry, uncle. Come! Dine with us tomorrow."

Scrooge said that he would see him -- yes, indeed he did. He went the whole length of the expression, and said that he would see him in that extremity first.

"But why?" cried Scrooge's nephew. "Why?"

"Why did you get married?" said Scrooge.

"Because I fell in love."

"Because you fell in love!" growled Scrooge, as if that were the only one thing in the world more ridiculous than a merry Christmas. "Good afternoon!"

"Nay, uncle, but you never came to see me before that happened. Why give it as a reason for not coming now?"

"Good afternoon," said Scrooge.

"I want nothing from you; I ask nothing of you; why cannot we be friends?"

"Good afternoon," said Scrooge.

"I am sorry, with all my heart, to find you so resolute. We have never had any quarrel, to which I have been a party. But I have made the trial in homage to Christmas, and I'll keep my Christmas humour to the last. So A Merry Christmas, uncle!"

"Good afternoon," said Scrooge.

"And A Happy New Year!"

"Good afternoon!" said Scrooge.

His nephew left the room without an angry word, notwithstanding. He stopped at the outer door to bestow the greetings of the season on the clerk, who cold as he was, was warmer than Scrooge; for he returned them cordially.

"There's another fellow," muttered Scrooge; who overheard him: "my clerk, with fifteen shillings a week, and a wife and family, talking about a merry Christmas. I'll retire to Bedlam."

This lunatic, in letting Scrooge's nephew out, had let two other people in. They were portly gentlemen, pleasant to behold, and now stood, with their hats off, in Scrooge's office. They had books and papers in their hands, and bowed to him.

"Scrooge and Marley's, I believe," said one of the gentlemen, referring to his list. "Have I the pleasure of addressing Mr. Scrooge, or Mr. Marley?"

"Mr. Marley has been dead these seven years," Scrooge replied. "He died seven years ago, this very night."

"We have no doubt his liberality is well represented by his surviving partner," said the gentleman, presenting his credentials.

It certainly was; for they had been two kindred spirits. At the ominous word "liberality," Scrooge frowned, and shook his head, and handed the credentials back.

"At this festive season of the year, Mr. Scrooge," said the gentleman, taking up a pen, "it is more than usually desirable that we should make some slight provision for the Poor and Destitute, who suffer greatly at the present time. Many thousands are in want of common necessaries; hundreds of thousands are in want of common comforts, sir."

"Are there no prisons?" asked Scrooge.

"Plenty of prisons," said the gentleman, laying down the pen again.

"And the Union workhouses?" demanded Scrooge. "Are they still in operation?"

"They are. Still," returned the gentleman, "I wish I could say they were not."

"The Treadmill and the Poor Law are in full vigour, then?" said Scrooge.

"Both very busy, sir."

"Oh! I was afraid, from what you said at first, that something had occurred to stop them in their useful course," said Scrooge. "I'm very glad to hear it."

"Under the impression that they scarcely furnish Christian cheer of mind or body to the multitude," returned the gentleman, "a few of us are endeavouring to raise a fund to buy the Poor some meat and drink and means of warmth. We choose this time, because it is a time, of all others, when Want is keenly felt, and Abundance rejoices. What shall I put you down for?"

"Nothing!" Scrooge replied.

"You wish to be anonymous?"

"I wish to be left alone," said Scrooge. "Since you ask me what I wish, gentlemen, that is my answer. I don't make merry myself at Christmas and I can't afford to make idle people merry. I help to support the establishments I have mentioned -- they cost enough; and those who are badly off must go there."

"Many can't go there; and many would rather die."

"If they would rather die," said Scrooge, "they had better do it, and decrease the surplus population. Besides -- excuse me -- I don't know that."

"But you might know it," observed the gentleman.

"It's not my business," Scrooge returned. "It's enough for a man to understand his own business, and not to interfere with other people's. Mine occupies me constantly. Good afternoon, gentlemen!"

Seeing clearly that it would be useless to pursue their point, the gentlemen withdrew. Scrooge returned his labours with an improved opinion of himself, and in a more facetious temper than was usual with him.

Meanwhile the fog and darkness thickened so, that people ran about with flaring links, proffering their services to go before horses in carriages, and conduct them on their way. The ancient tower of a church, whose gruff old bell was always peeping slyly down at Scrooge out of a Gothic window in the wall, became invisible, and struck the hours and quarters in the clouds, with tremulous vibrations afterwards as if its teeth were chattering in its frozen head up there. The cold became intense. In the main street at the corner of the court, some labourers were repairing the gas-pipes, and had lighted a great fire in a brazier, round which a party of ragged men and boys were gathered: warming their hands and winking their eyes before the blaze in rapture. The water-plug being left in solitude, its overflowing sullenly congealed, and turned to misanthropic ice. The brightness of the shops where holly sprigs and berries crackled in the lamp heat of the windows, made pale faces ruddy as they passed. Poulterers' and grocers' trades became a splendid joke; a glorious pageant, with which it was next to impossible to believe that such dull principles as bargain and sale had anything to do. The Lord Mayor, in the stronghold of the mighty Mansion House, gave orders to his fifty cooks and butlers to keep Christmas as a Lord Mayor's household should; and even the little tailor, whom he had fined five shillings on the previous Monday for being drunk and bloodthirsty in the streets, stirred up to-morrow's pudding in his garret, while his lean wife and the baby sallied out to buy the beef.

Foggier yet, and colder! Piercing, searching, biting cold. If the good Saint Dunstan had but nipped the Evil Spirit's nose with a touch of such weather as that, instead of using his familiar weapons, then indeed he would have roared to lusty purpose. The owner of one scant young nose, gnawed and mumbled by the hungry cold as bones are gnawed by dogs, stooped down at Scrooge's keyhole to regale him with a Christmas carol: but at the first sound of --

"God bless you, merry gentleman! May nothing you dismay!"

Scrooge seized the ruler with such energy of action, that the singer fled in terror, leaving the keyhole to the fog and even more congenial frost.

At length the hour of shutting up the counting house arrived. With an ill-will Scrooge dismounted from his stool, and tacitly admitted the fact to the expectant clerk in the Tank, who instantly snuffed his candle out, and put on his hat.

"You'll want all day to-morrow, I suppose?" said Scrooge.

"If quite convenient, sir."

"It's not convenient," said Scrooge, "and it's not fair. If I was to stop half-a-crown for it, you'd think yourself ill-used, I'll be bound?"

The clerk smiled faintly.

"And yet," said Scrooge, "you don't think me ill-used, when I pay a day's wages for no work."

The clerk observed that it was only once a year.

"A poor excuse for picking a man's pocket every twenty-fifth of December!" said Scrooge, buttoning his great-coat to the chin. "But I suppose you must have the whole day. Be here all the earlier next morning."

The clerk promised that he would; and Scrooge walked out with a growl. The office was closed in a twinkling, and the clerk, with the long ends of his white comforter dangling below his waist (for he boasted no great-coat), went down a slide on Cornhill, at the end of a lane of boys, twenty times, in honour of its being Christmas Eve, and then ran home to Camden Town as hard as he could pelt, to play at blindman's-buff.

Scrooge took his melancholy dinner in his usual melancholy tavern; and having read all the newspapers, and beguiled the rest of the evening with his banker's-book, went home to bed. He lived in chambers which had once belonged to his deceased partner. They were a gloomy suite of rooms, in a lowering pile of building up a yard, where it had so little business to be, that one could scarcely help fancying it must have run there when it was a young house, playing at hide-and-seek with other houses, and forgotten the way out again. It was old enough now, and dreary enough, for nobody lived in it but Scrooge, the other rooms being all let out as offices. The yard was so dark that even Scrooge, who knew its every stone, was fain to grope with his hands. The fog and frost so hung about the black old gateway of the house, that it seemed as if the Genius of the Weather sat in mournful meditation on the threshold.

Now, it is a fact, that there was nothing at all particular about the knocker on the door, except that it was very large. It is also a fact, that Scrooge had seen it, night and morning, during his whole residence in that place; also that Scrooge had as little of what is called fancy about him as any man in the city of London, even including -- which is a bold word -- the corporation, aldermen, and livery. Let it also be borne in mind that Scrooge had not bestowed one thought on Marley, since his last mention of his seven years' dead partner that afternoon. And then let any man explain to me, if he can, how it happened that Scrooge, having his key in the lock of the door, saw in the knocker, without its undergoing any intermediate process of change -- not a knocker, but Marley's face.

Marley's face. It was not in impenetrable shadow as the other objects in the yard were, but had a dismal light about it, like a bad lobster in a dark cellar. It was not angry or ferocious, but looked at Scrooge as Marley used to look: with ghostly spectacles turned up on its ghostly forehead. The hair was curiously stirred, as if by breath or hot air; and, though the eyes were wide open, they were perfectly motionless. That, and its livid colour, made it horrible; but its horror seemed to be in spite of the face and beyond its control, rather than a part or its own expression.

As Scrooge looked fixedly at this phenomenon, it was a knocker again.

To say that he was not startled, or that his blood was not conscious of a terrible sensation to which it had been a stranger from infancy, would be untrue. But he put his hand upon the key he had relinquished, turned it sturdily, walked in, and lighted his candle.

He did pause, with a moment's irresolution, before he shut the door; and he did look cautiously behind it first, as if he half-expected to be terrified with the sight of Marley's pigtail sticking out into the hall. But there was nothing on the back of the door, except the screws and nuts that held the knocker on, so he said "Pooh, pooh!" and closed it with a bang.

The sound resounded through the house like thunder. Every room above, and every cask in the wine-merchant's cellars below, appeared to have a separate peal of echoes of its own. Scrooge was not a man to be frightened by echoes. He fastened the door, and walked across the hall, and up the stairs; slowly too: trimming his candle as he went.

You may talk vaguely about driving a coach-and-six up a good old flight of stairs, or through a bad young Act of Parliament; but I mean to say you might have got a hearse up that staircase, and taken it broadwise, with the splinter-bar towards the wall and the door towards the balustrades: and done it easy. There was plenty of width for that, and room to spare; which is perhaps the reason why Scrooge thought he saw a locomotive hearse going on before him in the gloom. Half a dozen gas-lamps out of the street wouldn't have lighted the entry too well, so you may suppose that it was pretty dark with Scrooge's dip.

Up Scrooge went, not caring a button for that. Darkness is cheap, and Scrooge liked it. But before he shut his heavy door, he walked through his rooms to see that all was right. He had just enough recollection of the face to desire to do that.

Sitting-room, bedroom, lumber-room. All as they should be. Nobody under the table, nobody under the sofa; a small fire in the grate; spoon and basin ready; and the little saucepan of gruel (Scrooge had a cold in his head) upon the hob. Nobody under the bed; nobody in the closet; nobody in his dressing-gown, which was hanging up in a suspicious attitude against the wall. Lumber-room as usual. Old fire-guards, old shoes, two fish-baskets, washing-stand on three legs, and a poker.

Quite satisfied, he closed his door, and locked himself in; double-locked himself in, which was not his custom. Thus secured against surprise, he took off his cravat; put on his dressing-gown and slippers, and his nightcap; and sat down before the fire to take his gruel.

It was a very low fire indeed; nothing on such a bitter night. He was obliged to sit close to it, and brood over it, before he could extract the least sensation of warmth from such a handful of fuel. The fireplace was an old one, built by some Dutch merchant long ago, and paved all round with quaint Dutch tiles, designed to illustrate the Scriptures. There were Cains and Abels, Pharaohs' daughters;

Queens of Sheba, Angelic messengers descending through the air on clouds like feather-beds, Abrahams, Belshazzars, Apostles putting off to sea in butter-boats, hundreds of figures to attract his thoughts -- and yet that face of Marley, seven years dead, came like the ancient Prophet's rod, and swallowed up the whole. If each smooth tile had been a blank at first, with power to shape some picture on its surface from the disjointed fragments of his thoughts, there would have been a copy of old Marley's head on every one.

"Humbug!" said Scrooge; and walked across the room.

After several turns, he sat down again. As he threw his head back in the chair, his glance happened to rest upon a bell, a disused bell, that hung in the room, and communicated for some purpose now forgotten with a chamber in the highest story of the building. It was with great astonishment, and with a strange, inexplicable dread, that as he looked, he saw this bell begin to swing. It swung so softly in the outset that it scarcely made a sound; but soon it rang out loudly, and so did every bell in the house.

This might have lasted half a minute, or a minute, but it seemed an hour. The bells ceased as they had begun, together. They were succeeded by a clanking noise, deep down below; as if some person were dragging a heavy chain over the casks in the wine merchant's cellar. Scrooge then remembered to have heard that ghosts in haunted houses were described as dragging chains.

The cellar-door flew open with a booming sound, and then he heard the noise much louder, on the floors below; then coming up the stairs; then coming straight towards his door.

"It's humbug still!" said Scrooge. "I won't believe it."

His colour changed though, when, without a pause, it came on through the heavy door, and passed into the room before his eyes. Upon its coming in, the dying flame leaped up, as though it cried, "I know him; Marley's Ghost!" and fell again.

The same face: the very same. Marley in his pigtail, usual waistcoat, tights and boots; the tassels on the latter bristling, like his pigtail, and his coat-skirts, and the hair upon his head. The chain he drew was clasped about his middle. It was long, and wound about him like a tail; and it was made (for Scrooge observed it closely) of cash-boxes, keys, padlocks, ledgers, deeds, and heavy purses wrought in steel. His body was transparent, so that Scrooge, observing him, and looking through his waistcoat, could see the two buttons on his coat behind.

Scrooge had often heard it said that Marley had no bowels, but he had never believed it until now.

No, nor did he believe it even now. Though he looked the phantom through and through, and saw it standing before him; though he felt the chilling influence of its death-cold eyes; and marked the very texture of the folded kerchief bound about its head and chin, which wrapper he had not observed before: he was still incredulous, and fought against his senses.

"How now!" said Scrooge, caustic and cold as ever. "What do you want with me?"

"Much!" -- Marley's voice, no doubt about it.

"Who are you?"

"Ask me who I *was.*"

"Who *were* you then?" said Scrooge, raising his voice. "You're particular, for a shade." He was going to say "*to* a shade," but substituted this, as more appropriate.

"In life I was your partner, Jacob Marley."

"Can you -- can you sit down?" asked Scrooge, looking doubtfully at him.

"I can."

"Do it then."

Scrooge asked the question, because he didn't know whether a ghost so transparent might find himself in a condition to take a chair; and felt that in the event of its being impossible, it might involve the necessity of an embarrassing explanation. But the ghost sat down on the opposite side of the fireplace, as if he were quite used to it.

"You don't believe in me," observed the Ghost.

"I don't." said Scrooge.

"What evidence would you have of my reality, beyond that of your senses?"

"I don't know," said Scrooge.

"Why do you doubt your senses?"

"Because," said Scrooge, "a little thing affects them. A slight disorder of the stomach makes them cheats. You may be an undigested bit of beef, a blot of mustard, a crumb of cheese, a fragment of an underdone potato. There's more of gravy than of grave about you, whatever you are!"

Scrooge was not much in the habit of cracking jokes, nor did he feel, in his heart, by any means waggish then. The truth is, that he tried to be smart, as a means of distracting his own attention, and keeping down his terror; for the spectre's voice disturbed the very marrow in his bones.

To sit, staring at those fixed glazed eyes, in silence for a moment, would play, Scrooge felt, the very deuce with him. There was something very awful, too, in the spectre's being provided with an infernal atmosphere of its own. Scrooge could not feel it himself, but this was clearly the case; for though the Ghost sat perfectly motionless, its hair, and skirts, and tassels, were still agitated as by the hot vapour from an oven.

"You see this toothpick?" said Scrooge, returning quickly to the charge, for the reason just assigned; and wishing, though it were only for a second, to divert the vision's stony gaze from himself.

"I do," replied the Ghost.

"You are not looking at it," said Scrooge.

"But I see it," said the Ghost, "notwithstanding."

"Well!" returned Scrooge, "I have but to swallow this, and be for the rest of my days persecuted by a legion of goblins, all of my own creation. Humbug, I tell you! humbug!"

At this the spirit raised a frightful cry, and shook its chain with such a dismal and appalling noise, that Scrooge held on tight to his chair, to save himself from falling in a swoon. But how much greater was his horror, when the phantom taking off the bandage round its head, as if it were too warm to wear indoors, its lower jaw dropped down upon its breast!

Scrooge fell upon his knees, and clasped his hands before his face.

"Mercy!" he said. "Dreadful apparition, why do you trouble me?"

"Man of the worldly mind!" replied the Ghost, "do you believe in me or not?"

"I do," said Scrooge. "I must. But why do spirits walk the earth, and why do they come to me?"

"It is required of every man," the Ghost returned, "that the spirit within him should walk abroad among his fellowmen, and travel far and wide; and if that spirit goes not forth in life, it is condemned to do so after death. It is doomed to wander through the world -- oh, woe is me! -- and witness what it cannot share, but might have shared on earth, and turned to happiness!"

Again the spectre raised a cry, and shook its chain and wrung its shadowy hands.

"You are fettered," said Scrooge, trembling. "Tell me why?"

"I wear the chain I forged in life," replied the Ghost. "I made it link by link, and yard by yard; I girded it on of my own free will, and of my own free will I wore it. Is its pattern strange to you?"

Scrooge trembled more and more.

"Or would you know," pursued the Ghost, "the weight and length of the strong coil you bear yourself? It was full as heavy and as long as this, seven Christmas Eves ago. You have laboured on it, since. It is a ponderous chain!"

Scrooge glanced about him on the floor, in the expectation of finding himself surrounded by some fifty or sixty fathoms of iron cable: but he could see nothing.

"Jacob," he said, imploringly. "Old Jacob Marley, tell me more. Speak comfort to me, Jacob!"

"I have none to give," the Ghost replied. "It comes from other regions, Ebenezer Scrooge, and is conveyed by other ministers, to other kinds of men. Nor can I tell you what I would. A very little more, is all permitted to me. I cannot rest, I cannot stay, I cannot linger anywhere. My spirit never walked beyond our counting-house -- mark me! -- in life my spirit never roved beyond the narrow limits of our money-changing hole; and weary journeys lie before me!"

It was a habit with Scrooge, whenever he became thoughtful, to put his hands in his breeches pockets. Pondering on what the Ghost had said, he did so now, but without lifting up his eyes, or getting off his knees.

"You must have been very slow about it, Jacob," Scrooge observed, in a business-like manner, though with humility and deference.

"Slow!" the Ghost repeated.

"Seven years dead," mused Scrooge. "And travelling all the time!"

"The whole time," said the Ghost. "No rest, no peace. Incessant torture of remorse."

"You travel fast?" said Scrooge.

"On the wings of the wind," replied the Ghost.

"You might have got over a great quantity of ground in seven years," said Scrooge.

The Ghost, on hearing this, set up another cry, and clanked its chain so hideously in the dead silence of the night, that the Ward would have been justified in indicting it for a nuisance.

"Oh! captive, bound, and double-ironed," cried the phantom, "not to know, that ages of incessant labour, by immortal creatures, for this earth must pass into eternity before the good of which it is susceptible is all developed. Not to know that any Christian spirit working kindly in its little sphere, whatever it may be, will find its mortal life too short for its vast means of usefulness. Not to know that no space of regret can make amends for one life's opportunity misused! Yet such was I! Oh! such was I!"

"But you were always a good man of business, Jacob," faltered Scrooge, who now began to apply this to himself.

"Business!" cried the Ghost, wringing its hands again. "Mankind was my business. The common welfare was my business; charity, mercy, forbearance, and benevolence, were, all, my business. The dealings of my trade were but a drop of water in the comprehensive ocean of my business!"

It held up its chain at arm's length, as if that were the cause of all its unavailing grief, and flung it heavily upon the ground again.

"At this time of the rolling year," the spectre said "I suffer most. Why did I walk through crowds of fellow-beings with my eyes turned down, and never raise them to that blessed Star which led the Wise Men to a poor abode! Were there no poor homes to which its light would have conducted me!"

Scrooge was very much dismayed to hear the spectre going on at this rate, and began to quake exceedingly.

"Hear me!" cried the Ghost. "My time is nearly gone."

"I will," said Scrooge. "But don't be hard upon me! Don't be flowery, Jacob! Pray!"

"How it is that I appear before you in a shape that you can see, I may not tell. I have sat invisible beside you many and many a day."

It was not an agreeable idea. Scrooge shivered, and wiped the perspiration from his brow.

"That is no light part of my penance," pursued the Ghost. "I am here to-night to warn you, that you have yet a chance and hope of escaping my fate. A chance and hope of my procuring, Ebenezer."

"You were always a good friend to me," said Scrooge. "Thank `ee!"

"You will be haunted," resumed the Ghost, "by Three Spirits."

Scrooge's countenance fell almost as low as the Ghost's had done.

"Is that the chance and hope you mentioned, Jacob?" he demanded, in a faltering voice.

"It is."

"I -- I think I'd rather not," said Scrooge.

"Without their visits," said the Ghost, "you cannot hope to shun the path I tread. Expect the first tomorrow, when the bell tolls one."

"Couldn't I take `em all at once, and have it over, Jacob?" hinted Scrooge.

"Expect the second on the next night at the same hour. The third upon the next night when the last stroke of twelve has ceased to vibrate. Look to see me no more; and look that, for your own sake, you remember what has passed between us!"

When it had said these words, the spectre took its wrapper from the table, and bound it round its head, as before. Scrooge knew this, by the smart sound its teeth made, when the jaws were brought together by the bandage. He ventured to raise his eyes again, and found his supernatural visitor confronting him in an erect attitude, with its chain wound over and about its arm.

The apparition walked backward from him; and at every step it took, the window raised itself a little, so that when the spectre reached it, it was wide open. It beckoned Scrooge to approach, which he did. When they were within two paces of each other, Marley's Ghost held up its hand, warning him to come no nearer. Scrooge stopped.

Not so much in obedience, as in surprise and fear: for on the raising of the hand, he became sensible of confused noises in the air; incoherent sounds of lamentation and regret; wailings inexpressibly sorrowful and self-accusatory. The spectre, after listening for a moment, joined in the mournful dirge; and floated out upon the bleak, dark night.

Scrooge followed to the window: desperate in his curiosity. He looked out.

The air was filled with phantoms, wandering hither and thither in restless haste, and moaning as they went. Every one of them wore chains like Marley's Ghost; some few (they might be guilty governments) were linked together; none were free. Many had been personally known to Scrooge in their lives. He had been quite familiar with one old ghost, in a white waistcoat, with a monstrous iron safe attached to its ankle, who cried piteously at being unable to assist a wretched woman with an infant, whom it saw below, upon a door-step. The misery with them all was, clearly, that they sought to interfere, for good, in human matters, and had lost the power for ever.

Whether these creatures faded into mist, or mist enshrouded them, he could not tell. But they and their spirit voices faded together; and the night became as it had been when he walked home.

Scrooge closed the window, and examined the door by which the Ghost had entered. It was double-locked, as he had locked it with his own hands, and the bolts were undisturbed. He tried to say "Humbug!" but stopped at the first syllable. And being, from the emotion he had undergone, or the fatigues of the day, or his glimpse of the Invisible World, or the dull conversation of the Ghost, or the lateness of the hour, much in need of repose; went straight to bed, without undressing, and fell asleep upon the instant.

You can find the video on YouTube at:
http://www.youtube.com/playlist?list=PL8746E94BD967E77F

Meta Model Challenge

This lesson's Meta Model trap is called, "I don't know." This challenge is more often heard in speaking than seen in the written word. It is good to recognize it and know what to do when someone says it to you. You can help the person gain clarity in his/her thinking. Here is a typical sentence.

I do not know about the book, "The Christmas Carol."

What is it that you do not know?

If you did know, what would you know?

What is it that you want to know about the book?

A sample answer might be, I do know if the old book, "A Christmas Carol" is worth reading since it was written so many years ago.

Lesson 14: A Christmas Carol and Character Analysis

Homework Assignment

Fill out the chart. You many use 2-3 words for each level. Then use the information from the chart to write a short essay about the person you chose. Print out your essay for next week. Remember a title. It is acceptable in this assignment to take a little "poetic license" to fill in the chart or to leave a part blank if you cannot come up with an answer.

Choose one: young Scrooge, Fan, Belle, Fezziwig, or Marley You may not be able to do every level, just do what you can.	
Environment	
Behavior	
Capability	
Beliefs/Values	
Identity	
Purpose	

Weekly Reading -- Christmas Carol

CHRISTMAS CAROL by Charles Dickens

Stave 2: The First of the Three Spirits

When Scrooge awoke, it was so dark, that looking out of bed, he could scarcely distinguish the transparent window from the opaque walls of his chamber. He was endeavouring to pierce the darkness with his ferret eyes, when the chimes of a neighbouring church struck the four quarters. So he listened for the hour.

To his great astonishment the heavy bell went on from six to seven, and from seven to eight, and regularly up to twelve; then stopped. Twelve. It was past two when he went to bed. The clock was wrong. An icicle must have got into the works. Twelve.

He touched the spring of his repeater, to correct this most preposterous clock. Its rapid little pulse beat twelve: and stopped.

"Why, it isn't possible," said Scrooge, "that I can have slept through a whole day and far into another night. It isn't possible that anything has happened to the sun, and this is twelve at noon."

The idea being an alarming one, he scrambled out of bed, and groped his way to the window. He was obliged to rub the frost off with the sleeve of his dressing-gown before he could see anything; and could see very little then. All he could make out was, that it was still very foggy and extremely cold, and that there was no noise of people running to and fro, and making a great stir, as there unquestionably would have been if night had beaten off bright day, and taken possession of the world. This was a great relief, because "three days after sight of this First of Exchange pay to Mr. . Ebenezer Scrooge or his order," and so forth, would have become a mere United States' security if there were no days to count by.

Scrooge went to bed again, and thought, and thought, and thought it over and over and over, and could make nothing of it. The more he thought, the more perplexed he was; and the more he endeavored not to think, the more he thought. Marley's Ghost bothered him exceedingly. Every time he resolved within himself, after mature inquiry, that it was all a dream, his mind flew back again, like a strong spring released, to its first position, and presented the same problem to be worked all through, "Was it a dream or not?"

Scrooge lay in this state until the chimes had gone three quarters more, when he remembered, on a sudden, that the Ghost had warned him of a visitation when the bell tolled one. He resolved to lie awake until the hour was past; and, considering that he could no more go to sleep than go to Heaven, this was perhaps the wisest resolution in his power.

The quarter was so long, that he was more than once convinced he must have sunk into a doze unconsciously, and missed the clock. At length it broke upon his listening ear.

"Ding, dong!"

"A quarter past," said Scrooge, counting.

"Ding dong!"

"Half past!" said Scrooge.

"Ding dong!"

"A quarter to it," said Scrooge.

"Ding dong!"

"The hour itself," said Scrooge, triumphantly,

"and nothing else!"

He spoke before the hour bell sounded, which it now did with a deep, dull, hollow, melancholy One. Light flashed up in the room upon the instant, and the curtains of his bed were drawn.

The curtains of his bed were drawn aside, I tell you, by a hand. Not the curtains at his feet, nor the curtains at his back, but those to which his face was addressed. The curtains of his bed were drawn aside; and Scrooge, starting up into a half-recumbent attitude, found himself face to face with the unearthly visitor who drew them: as close to it as I am now to you, and I am standing in the spirit at your elbow.

It was a strange figure -- like a child: yet not so like a child as like an old man, viewed through some supernatural medium, which gave him the appearance of having receded from the view, and being diminished to a child's proportions. Its hair, which hung about its neck and down its back, was white as if with age; and yet the face had not a wrinkle in it, and the tenderest bloom was on the skin. The arms were very long and muscular; the hands the same, as if its hold were of uncommon strength. Its legs and feet, most delicately formed, were, like those upper members, bare. It wore a tunic of the purest white, and round its waist was bound a lustrous belt, the sheen of which was beautiful. It held a branch of fresh green holly in its hand; and, in singular contradiction of that wintry emblem, had its dress trimmed with summer flowers. But the strangest thing about it was, that from the crown of its head there sprung a bright clear jet of light, by which all this was visible;

and which was doubtless the occasion of its using, in its duller moments, a great extinguisher for a cap, which it now held under its arm.

Even this, though, when Scrooge looked at it with increasing steadiness, was not its strangest quality. For as its belt sparkled and glittered now in one part and now in another, and what was light one instant, at another time was dark, so the figure itself fluctuated in its distinctness: being now a thing with one arm, now with one leg, now with twenty legs, now a pair of legs without a head, now a head without a body: of which dissolving parts, no outline would be visible in the dense gloom wherein they melted away. And in the very wonder of this, it would be itself again; distinct and clear as ever.

"Are you the Spirit, sir, whose coming was foretold to me?" asked Scrooge.

"I am."

The voice was soft and gentle. Singularly low, as if instead of being so close beside him, it were at a distance.

"Who, and what are you?" Scrooge demanded.

"I am the Ghost of Christmas Past."

"Long Past?" inquired Scrooge: observant of its dwarfish stature.

"No. Your past."

Perhaps, Scrooge could not have told anybody why, if anybody could have asked him; but he had a special desire to see the Spirit in his cap; and begged him to be covered.

"What!" exclaimed the Ghost, "Would you so soon put out, with worldly hands, the light I give? Is it not enough that you are one of those whose passions made this cap, and force me through whole trains of years to wear it low upon my brow!"

Scrooge reverently disclaimed all intention to offend or any knowledge of having willfully bonneted the Spirit at any period of his life. He then made bold to inquire what business brought him there.

"Your welfare," said the Ghost.

Scrooge expressed himself much obliged, but could not help thinking that a night of unbroken rest would have been more conducive to that end. The Spirit must have heard him thinking, for it said immediately:

"Your reclamation, then. Take heed."

It put out its strong hand as it spoke, and clasped him gently by the arm.

"Rise. And walk with me."

It would have been in vain for Scrooge to plead that the weather and the hour were not adapted to pedestrian purposes; that bed was warm, and the thermometer a long way below freezing; that he was clad but lightly in his slippers, dressing-gown, and nightcap; and that he had a cold upon him at that time. The grasp, though gentle as a woman's hand, was not to be resisted. He rose: but finding that the Spirit made towards the window, clasped his robe in supplication.

"I am mortal," Scrooge remonstrated, "and liable to fall."

"Bear but a touch of my hand there," said the Spirit, laying it upon his heart, "and you shall be upheld in more than this."

As the words were spoken, they passed through the wall, and stood upon an open country road, with fields on either hand. The city had entirely vanished. Not a vestige of it was to be seen. The darkness and the mist had vanished with it, for it was a clear, cold, winter day, with snow upon the ground.

"Good Heaven!" said Scrooge, clasping his hands together, as he looked about him. "I was bred in this place. I was a boy here."

The Spirit gazed upon him mildly. Its gentle touch, though it had been light and instantaneous, appeared still present to the old man's sense of feeling. He was conscious of a thousand odours floating in the air, each one connected with a thousand thoughts, and hopes, and joys, and cares long, long, forgotten.

"Your lip is trembling," said the Ghost. "And what is that upon your cheek?"

Scrooge muttered, with an unusual catching in his voice, that it was a pimple; and begged the Ghost to lead him where he would.

"You recollect the way?" inquired the Spirit.

"Remember it!" cried Scrooge with fervour -- "I could walk it blindfold."

"Strange to have forgotten it for so many years," observed the Ghost. "Let us go on."

They walked along the road, Scrooge recognising every gate, and post, and tree; until a little market-town appeared in the distance, with its bridge, its church, and winding river. Some shaggy ponies now were seen trotting towards them with boys upon their backs, who called to other boys in country gigs and carts, driven by farmers. All these boys were in great spirits, and shouted to each other, until the broad fields were so full of merry music, that the crisp air laughed to hear it.

"These are but shadows of the things that have been," said the Ghost. "They have no consciousness of us."

The jocund travellers came on; and as they came, Scrooge knew and named them every one. Why was he rejoiced beyond all bounds to see them. Why did his cold eye glisten, and his heart leap up as they went past? Why was he filled with gladness when he heard them give each other Merry Christmas, as they parted at cross-roads and-bye ways, for their several homes? What was merry Christmas to Scrooge? Out upon merry Christmas! What good had it ever done to him?

"The school is not quite deserted," said the Ghost. "A solitary child, neglected by his friends, is left there still."

Scrooge said he knew it. And he sobbed.

They left the high-road, by a well-remembered lane, and soon approached a mansion of dull red brick, with a little weathercock-surmounted cupola, on the roof, and a bell hanging in it. It was a large house, but one of broken fortunes; for the spacious offices were little used, their walls were damp and mossy, their windows broken, and their gates decayed. Fowls clucked and strutted in the stables; and the coach-houses and sheds were over-run with grass. Nor was it more retentive of its ancient state, within; for entering the dreary hall, and glancing through the open doors of many rooms, they found them poorly furnished, cold, and vast. There was an earthy savour in the air, a chilly bareness in the place, which associated itself somehow with too much getting up by candle-light, and not too much to eat.

They went, the Ghost and Scrooge, across the hall, to a door at the back of the house. It opened before them, and disclosed a long, bare, melancholy room, made barer still by lines of plain deal forms and desks. At one of these a lonely boy was reading near a feeble fire; and Scrooge sat down upon a form, and wept to see his poor forgotten self as he used to be.

Not a latent echo in the house, not a squeak and scuffle from the mice behind the paneling, not a drip from the half-thawed water-spout in the dull yard behind, not a sigh among the leafless boughs of one despondent poplar, not the idle swinging of an empty store-house door, no, not a clicking in the fire, but fell upon the heart of Scrooge with a softening influence, and gave a freer passage to his tears.

The Spirit touched him on the arm, and pointed to his younger self, intent upon his reading. Suddenly a man, in foreign garments: wonderfully real and distinct to look at: stood outside the window, with an ax stuck in his belt, and leading by the bridle an ass laden with wood.

"Why, it's Ali Baba!" Scrooge exclaimed in ecstasy. "It's dear old honest Ali Baba. Yes, yes, I know. One Christmas time, when yonder solitary child was left here all alone, he did come, for the first time, just like that. Poor boy. And Valentine," said Scrooge, "and his wild brother, Orson; there they go. And what's his name, who was put down in his drawers, asleep, at the Gate of Damascus; don't you see him? And the Sultan's Groom turned upside down by the Genii; there he is upon his head. Serve him right. I'm glad of it. What business had he to be married to the Princess."

To hear Scrooge expending all the earnestness of his nature on such subjects, in a most extraordinary voice between laughing and crying; and to see his heightened and excited face; would have been a surprise to his business friends in the city, indeed.

"There's the Parrot." cried Scrooge. "Green body and yellow tail, with a thing like a lettuce growing out of the top of his head; there he is! Poor Robin Crusoe, he called him, when he came home again after sailing round the island. "Poor Robin Crusoe, where have you been, Robin Crusoe?" The man thought he was dreaming, but he wasn't. It was the Parrot, you know. There goes Friday, running for his life to the little creek! Halloa! Hoop! Hallo!"

Then, with a rapidity of transition very foreign to his usual character, he said, in pity for his former self, "Poor boy!" and cried again.

"I wish," Scrooge muttered, putting his hand in his pocket, and looking about him, after drying his eyes with his cuff: "but it's too late now."

"What is the matter?" asked the Spirit.

"Nothing," said Scrooge. "Nothing. There was a boy singing a Christmas Carol at my door last night. I should like to have given him something: that's all."

The Ghost smiled thoughtfully, and waved its hand: saying as it did so, "Let us see another Christmas!"

Scrooge's former self grew larger at the words, and the room became a little darker and more dirty. The panels shrunk, the windows cracked; fragments of plaster fell out of the ceiling, and the naked laths were shown instead; but how all this was brought about, Scrooge knew no more than you do. He only knew that it was quite correct; that everything had happened so; that there he was, alone again, when all the other boys had gone home for the jolly holidays.

He was not reading now, but walking up and down despairingly. Scrooge looked at the Ghost, and with a mournful shaking of his head, glanced anxiously towards the door.

It opened; and a little girl, much younger than the boy, came darting in, and putting her arms about his neck, and often kissing him, addressed him as her "Dear, dear brother."

"I have come to bring you home, dear brother!" said the child, clapping her tiny hands, and bending down to laugh. "To bring you home, home, home!"

"Home, little Fan?" returned the boy.

"Yes!" said the child, brimful of glee. "Home, for good and all. Home, for ever and ever. Father is so much kinder than he used to be, that home's like Heaven! He spoke so gently to me one dear night when I was going to bed, that I was not afraid to ask him once more if you might come home; and he said Yes, you should; and sent me in a coach to bring you. And you're to be a man!" said the child, opening her eyes, "and are never to come back here; but first, we're to be together all the Christmas long, and have the merriest time in all the world."

"You are quite a woman, little Fan!"exclaimed the boy.

She clapped her hands and laughed, and tried to touch his head; but being too little, laughed again, and stood on tiptoe to embrace him. Then she began to drag him, in her childish eagerness, towards the door; and he, nothing loth to go, accompanied her.

A terrible voice in the hall cried. "Bring down Master Scrooge's box, there!" And in the hall appeared the schoolmaster himself, who glared on Master Scrooge with a ferocious condescension, and threw him into a dreadful state of mind by shaking hands with him. He then conveyed him and his sister into the veriest old well of a shivering best-parlour that ever was seen, where the maps upon the wall, and the celestial and terrestrial globes in the windows, were waxy with cold. Here he produced a decanter of curiously light wine, and a block of curiously heavy cake, and administered installments of those dainties to the young people: at the same time, sending out a meagre servant to offer a glass of "something" to the postboy, who answered that he thanked the gentleman, but if it was the same tap as he had tasted before, he had rather not. Master Scrooge's trunk being by this time tied on to the top of the chaise, the children bade the schoolmaster good-bye right willingly; and getting into it, drove gaily down the garden-sweep: the quick wheels dashing the hoar-frost and snow from off the dark leaves of the evergreens like spray.

"Always a delicate creature, whom a breath might have withered," said the Ghost. "But she had a large heart!"

"So she had," cried Scrooge. "You're right. I'll not gainsay it, Spirit. God forbid!"

"She died a woman," said the Ghost, "and had, as I think, children."

"One child," Scrooge returned.

"True," said the Ghost. "Your nephew!"

Scrooge seemed uneasy in his mind; and answered briefly, "Yes."

Although they had but that moment left the school behind them, they were now in the busy thoroughfares of a city, where shadowy passengers passed and repassed; where shadowy carts and coaches battle for the way, and all the strife and tumult of a real city were. It was made plain enough, by the dressing of the shops, that here too it was Christmas time again; but it was evening, and the streets were lighted up.

The Ghost stopped at a certain warehouse door, and asked Scrooge if he knew it.

"Know it!" said Scrooge. "Was I apprenticed here?"

They went in. At sight of an old gentleman in a Welsh wig, sitting behind such a high desk, that if he had been two inches taller he must have knocked his head against the ceiling, Scrooge cried in great excitement:

"Why, it's old Fezziwig! Bless his heart; it's Fezziwig alive again!"

Old Fezziwig laid down his pen, and looked up at the clock, which pointed to the hour of seven. He rubbed his hands; adjusted his capacious waistcoat; laughed all over himself, from his shows to his organ of benevolence; and called out in a comfortable, oily, rich, fat, jovial voice:

"Yo ho, there! Ebenezer! Dick!"

Scrooge's former self, now grown a young man, came briskly in, accompanied by his fellow-prentice.

"Dick Wilkins, to be sure," said Scrooge to the Ghost. "Bless me, yes. There he is. He was very much attached to me, was Dick. Poor Dick. Dear, dear."

"Yo ho, my boys!" said Fezziwig. "No more work to-night. Christmas Eve, Dick. Christmas, Ebenezer. Let's have the shutters up," cried old Fezziwig, with a sharp clap of his hands, "before a man can say Jack Robinson."

You wouldn't believe how those two fellows went at it. They charged into the street with the shutters -- one, two, three -- had them up in their places -- four, five, six -- barred them and pinned then -- seven, eight, nine -- and came back before you could have got to twelve, panting like race-horses.

"Hilli-ho!" cried old Fezziwig, skipping down from the high desk, with wonderful agility. "Clear away, my lads, and let's have lots of room here. Hilli-ho, Dick! Chirrup, Ebenezer."

Clear away! There was nothing they wouldn't have cleared away, or couldn't have cleared away, with old Fezziwig looking on. It was done in a minute. Every movable was packed off, as if it were dismissed from public life for evermore; the floor was swept and watered, the lamps were trimmed, fuel was heaped upon the fire; and the warehouse was as snug, and warm, and dry, and bright a ball-room, as you would desire to see upon a winter's night.

In came a fiddler with a music-book, and went up to the lofty desk, and made an orchestra of it, and tuned like fifty stomach-aches. In came Mr. sFezziwig, one vast substantial smile. In came the three Miss Fezziwigs, beaming and lovable. In came the six young followers whose hearts they broke. In came all the young men and women employed in the business. In came the housemaid, with her cousin, the baker. In came the cook, with her brother's particular friend, the milkman. In came the boy from over the way, who was suspected of not having board enough from his master; trying to hide himself behind the girl from next door but one, who was proved to have had her ears pulled by her mistress. In they all came, one after another; some shyly, some boldly, some gracefully, some awkwardly, some pushing, some pulling; in they all came, anyhow and everyhow. Away they all went, twenty couple at once; hands half round and back again the other way; down the middle and up again; round and round in various stages of affectionate grouping; old top couple always turning up in the wrong place; new top couple starting off again, as soon as they got there; all top couples at last, and not a bottom one to help them. When this result was brought about, old Fezziwig, clapping his hands to stop the dance, cried out, "Well done!" and the fiddler plunged his hot face into a pot of porter, especially provided for that purpose. But scorning rest, upon his reappearance, he instantly began again, though there were no dancers yet, as if the other fiddler had been carried home, exhausted, on a shutter, and he were a bran-new man resolved to beat him out of sight, or perish.

There were more dances, and there were forfeits, and more dances, and there was cake, and there was negus, (mulled wine) and there was a great piece of Cold Roast, and there was a great piece of Cold Boiled, and there were mince-pies, and plenty of beer. But the great effect of the evening came after the Roast and Boiled, when the fiddler (an artful dog, mind! The sort of man who knew his business better than you or I could have told it him!) struck up "Sir Roger de Coverley." Then old Fezziwig stood out to dance with Mr. Fezziwig. Top couple too; with a good stiff piece of work cut out for them; three or four and twenty pair of partners; people who were not to be trifled with; people who *would* dance, and had no notion of walking.

But if they had been twice as many -- ah, four times -- old Fezziwig would have been a match for them, and so would Mr. s. Fezziwig. As to *her*, she was worthy to be his partner in every sense of the term. If that's not high praise, tell me higher, and I'll use it. A positive light appeared to issue from Fezziwig's calves. They shone in every part of the dance like moons. You couldn't have predicted, at any given time, what would have become of them next. And when old Fezziwig and Mr. s. Fezziwig had gone all through the dance; advance and retire, both hands to your partner, bow and curtsey, corkscrew, thread-the-needle, and back again to your place; Fezziwig cut -- cut so deftly, that he appeared to wink with his legs, and came upon his feet again without a stagger.

When the clock struck eleven, this domestic ball broke up. Mr. and Mr. s. Fezziwig took their stations, one on either side of the door, and shaking hands with every person individually as he or she went out, wished him or her a Merry Christmas. When everybody had retired but the two prentices, they did the same to them; and thus the cheerful voices died away, and the lads were left to their beds; which were under a counter in the back-shop.

During the whole of this time, Scrooge had acted like a man out of his wits. His heart and soul were in the scene, and with his former self. He corroborated everything, remembered everything, enjoyed everything, and underwent the strangest agitation. It was not until now, when the bright faces of his former self and Dick were turned from them, that he remembered the Ghost, and became conscious that it was looking full upon him, while the light upon its head burnt very clear.

"A small matter," said the Ghost, "to make these silly folks so full of gratitude."

"Small!" echoed Scrooge.

The Spirit signed to him to listen to the two apprentices, who were pouring out their hearts in praise of Fezziwig: and when he had done so, said,

"Why! Is it not! He has spent but a few pounds of your mortal money: three or four perhaps. Is that so much that he deserves this praise?"

"It isn't that," said Scrooge, heated by the remark, and speaking unconsciously like his former, not his latter, self. "It isn't that, Spirit. He has the power to render us happy or unhappy; to make our service light or burdensome; a pleasure or a toil. Say that his power lies in words and looks; in things so slight and insignificant that it is impossible to add and count them up: what then? The happiness he gives, is quite as great as if it cost a fortune."

He felt the Spirit's glance, and stopped.

"What is the matter?" asked the Ghost.

"Nothing in particular," said Scrooge.

"Something, I think?" the Ghost insisted.

"No," said Scrooge, "No. I should like to be able to say a word or two to my clerk just now! That's all."

His former self turned down the lamps as he gave utterance to the wish; and Scrooge and the Ghost again stood side by side in the open air.

"My time grows short," observed the Spirit. "Quick!"

This was not addressed to Scrooge, or to any one whom he could see, but it produced an immediate effect. For again Scrooge saw himself. He was older now; a man in the prime of life. His face had not the harsh and rigid lines of later years; but it had begun to wear the signs of care and avarice. There was an eager, greedy, restless motion in the eye, which showed the passion that had taken root, and where the shadow of the growing tree would fall.

He was not alone, but sat by the side of a fair young girl in a mourning-dress: in whose eyes there were tears, which sparkled in the light that shone out of the Ghost of Christmas Past.

"It matters little," she said, softly. "To you, very little. Another idol has displaced me; and if it can cheer and comfort you in time to come, as I would have tried to do, I have no just cause to grieve."

"What Idol has displaced you?" he rejoined.

"A golden one."

"This is the even-handed dealing of the world!" he said. "There is nothing on which it is so hard as poverty; and there is nothing it professes to condemn with such severity as the pursuit of wealth!"

"You fear the world too much," she answered, gently. "All your other hopes have merged into the hope of being beyond the chance of its sordid reproach. I have seen your nobler aspirations fall off one by one, until the master-passion, Gain, engrosses you. Have I not?"

"What then?" he retorted. "Even if I have grown so much wiser, what then? I am not changed towards you."

She shook her head.

"Am I?"

"Our contract is an old one. It was made when we were both poor and content to be so, until, in good season, we could improve our worldly fortune by our patient industry. You *are* changed. When it was made, you were another man."

"I was a boy," he said impatiently.

"Your own feeling tells you that you were not what you are," she returned. "I am. That which promised happiness when we were one in heart, is fraught with misery now that we are two. How often and how keenly I have thought of this, I will not say. It is enough that I *have* thought of it, and can release you."

"Have I ever sought release?"

"In words? No. Never."

"In what, then?"

"In a changed nature; in an altered spirit; in another atmosphere of life; another Hope as its great end. In everything that made my love of any worth or value in your sight. If this had never been between us," said the girl, looking mildly, but with steadiness, upon him; "tell me, would you seek me out and try to win me now? Ah, no!"

He seemed to yield to the justice of this supposition, in spite of himself. But he said with a struggle," You think not?"

"I would gladly think otherwise if I could," she answered, "Heaven knows. When *I* have learned a Truth like this, I know how strong and irresistible it must be. But if you were free to-day, to-morrow, yesterday, can even I believe that you would choose a dowerless girl -- you who, in your very confidence with her, weigh everything by Gain: or, choosing her, if for a moment you were false enough to your one guiding principle to do so, do I not know that your repentance and regret would surely follow? I do; and I release you. With a full heart, for the love of him you once were."

He was about to speak; but with her head turned from him, she resumed.

"You may -- the memory of what is past half makes me hope you will -- have pain in this. A very, very brief time, and you will dismiss the recollection of it, gladly, as an unprofitable dream, from which it happened well that you awoke. May you be happy in the life you have chosen."

She left him, and they parted.

"Spirit!" said Scrooge, "show me no more! Conduct me home. Why do you delight to torture me?"

"One shadow more!" exclaimed the Ghost.

"No more!" cried Scrooge! "No more, I don't wish to see it! Show me no more!"

But the relentless Ghost pinioned him in both his arms, and forced him to observe what happened next.

They were in another scene and place; a room, not very large or handsome, but full of comfort. Near to the winter fire sat a beautiful young girl, so like that last that Scrooge believed it was the same, until he saw *her*, now a comely matron, sitting opposite her daughter. The noise in this room was perfectly tumultuous, for there were more children there, than Scrooge in his agitated state of mind could count; and, unlike the celebrated herd in the poem, they were not forty children conducting themselves like one, but every child was conducting itself like forty. The consequences were uproarious beyond belief; but no one seemed to care; on the contrary, the mother and daughter laughed heartily, and enjoyed it very much; and the latter, soon beginning to mingle in the sports, got pillaged by the young brigands most ruthlessly. What would I not have given to one of them. Though I never could have been so rude, no, no! I wouldn't for the wealth of all the world have crushed that braided hair, and torn it down; and for the precious little shoe, I wouldn't have plucked it off, God bless my soul! to save my life. As to measuring her waist in sport, as they did, bold young brood, I couldn't have done it; I should have expected my arm to have grown round it for a punishment, and never come straight again. And yet I should have dearly liked, I own, to have touched her lips; to have questioned her, that she might have opened them; to have looked upon the lashes of her downcast eyes, and never raised a blush; to have let loose waves of hair, an inch of which would be a keepsake beyond price: in short, I should have liked, I do confess, to have had the lightest licence of a child, and yet to have been man enough to know its value.

But now a knocking at the door was heard, and such a rush immediately ensued that she with laughing face and plundered dress was borne towards it the centre of a flushed and boisterous group, just in time to greet the father, who came home attended by a man laden with Christmas toys and presents. Then the shouting and the struggling, and the onslaught that was made on the defenceless porter. The scaling him with chairs for ladders to dive into his pockets, despoil him of brown-paper parcels, hold on tight by his cravat, hug him round his neck, pommel his back, and kick his legs in irrepressible affection. The shouts of wonder and delight with which the development of every package was received. The terrible announcement that the baby had been taken in the act of putting a doll's frying-pan into his mouth, and was more than suspected of having swallowed a fictitious turkey, glued on a wooden platter. The immense relief of finding this a false alarm. The joy, and gratitude, and ecstasy. They are all indescribable alike. It is enough that by degrees the children and their emotions got out of the parlour, and by one stair at a time, up to the top of the house; where they went to bed, and so subsided.

And now Scrooge looked on more attentively than ever, when the master of the house, having his daughter leaning fondly on him, sat down with her and her mother at his own fireside; and when he thought that such another creature, quite as graceful and as full of promise, might have called him father, and been a spring-time in the haggard winter of his life, his sight grew very dim indeed.

"Belle," said the husband, turning to his wife with a smile, "I saw an old friend of yours this afternoon."

"Who was it?"

"Guess!"

"How can I? Tut, don't I know," she added in the same breath, laughing as he laughed. "Mr. . Scrooge."

"Mr. . Scrooge it was. I passed his office window; and as it was not shut up, and he had a candle inside, I could scarcely help seeing him. His partner lies upon the point of death, I hear; and there he sat alone. Quite alone in the world, I do believe."

"Spirit!" said Scrooge in a broken voice, "remove me from this place."

"I told you these were shadows of the things that have been," said the Ghost. "That they are what they are, do not blame me!"

"Remove me!" Scrooge exclaimed, "I cannot bear it!"

He turned upon the Ghost, and seeing that it looked upon him with a face, in which in some strange way there were fragments of all the faces it had shown him, wrestled with it.

"Leave me! Take me back. Haunt me no longer!"

In the struggle, if that can be called a struggle in which the Ghost with no visible resistance on its own part was undisturbed by any effort of its adversary, Scrooge observed that its light was burning high and bright; and dimly connecting that with its influence over him, he seized the extinguisher-cap, and by a sudden action pressed it down upon its head.

The Spirit dropped beneath it, so that the extinguisher covered its whole form; but though Scrooge pressed it down with all his force, he could not hide the light, which streamed from under it, in an unbroken flood upon the ground.

He was conscious of being exhausted, and overcome by an irresistible drowsiness; and, further, of being in his own bedroom. He gave the cap a parting squeeze, in which his hand relaxed; and had barely time to reel to bed, before he sank into a heavy sleep.

Reading

Earlier you were introduced the NLP Logical Level Alignment program as you created a pro/con essay. In this lesson we will use the same program in a completely different application, a character sketch. Gregory Bateson's work was used by Robert Dilts. Dilts noted that as people move from the bottom level of environment to the top level of purpose increasing more of a person's neurology becomes involved. The environment level is sensory. Our sensory system inputs to our brain what we see, hear, smell, taste and feel it the place in the place where we are at. Then in that environment we move and becomes involved as we relate to it. Take as a for instance a person in a room with a piano. It is merely a man and a piano and nothing more. The man can see, possibly hear, feel and even taste and smell the piano but nothing more. Movement is at a deeper neurological level than our sensory input for no longer are we just gathering information about our environment, we are now reacting to it. The man takes a finger and strikes a key. He may notice that sound arises but the key strikes are random and shapeless yet from those movements capabilities arise.

Behaviors do not have a plan or a strategy. They occur naturally. Capabilities reach deeper into out neurology. We plan and shape the behavior. The man begins to play the keys in such a way that sound arises. When we are capable of doing things we the gain beliefs and values about those things we do. As the sound arises the man reaches deeper still into the neurology of his system and believes that he can put the notes together in such a way that they are beautiful and he value the beauty of the melodies that arise – well most of the time. Children practicing when they want to be laying may not value it much.

The man may be playing the piano. Soon he believes he can make beautiful music. He likes the sound of the music and possibly other things the music might give him such as friends who like to listen, a parent who praises him or even the money he makes as a pianist.

These capacities, beliefs and values give rise an identity, who we are. The man becomes a pianist. He takes on that as a part of his identity. This sense of who we are organizes the levels below as who we are relates to what we believe and value, and that to our capabilities which arise from our behaviors that are a reaction to our environment and basic needs. There is an awareness of what Gregory Bateson called, “the pattern that connects” all of the levels together in a larger whole something bigger than ourselves. As we recognize who we are we begin to see outside of ourselves and take on a purpose that is greater than we are. Our pianist desires to make beautiful music for others. He desires to entertain, to sooth, to delight and even to ‘rock on’ the pearly keys.

Take, for another example, a loved baby.

	Answers	
Environment	**when and where?**	an infant, nurturing environment of his home, cared and nurtured.
Behavior	***What?***	kicks his legs
Capability	***How?***	realizes that he can kick his legs at will and control the kicking
Beliefs and values	***why?***	it becomes fun to kick, it feels good, it may shake a crib toy and cause something to rattle or wiggle
		Babies naturally value change and the ability to control something outside of self
Identity	**Who?**	I am a being that can make something happen
Purpose	**“For Whom or What”**	When I kick and shake my toys it makes my mother happy and she smiles and laughs with me

This week in our writing we will use the Logical Level Alignment program (LLA) (Sometimes called Neuro-Logical Level Alignment Program, NLLA) to create a character analysis essay. You may find that this form will assist you in organizing your essay and give it alignment so that it flows quickly as your write and serves you well.

Sample

Ghost of Christmas Past	
Environment	The home of Ebenezer Scrooge in the 19th century
Behavior	gentle, childlike manner and yet old,
capability	wise and determined to make a change
Beliefs/Values	It is important to change Scrooge
Identity	I am a ghost who can make a change in someone's life
Purpose	Make life better for many people by changing Scrooge

Opening statement: Who you chose.

What kind of a person is he/she/it?

Why is s\he\it what s/he/it is?

I found the Ghost of Christmas Past an interesting character. The story takes place in old England during the middle of the 19th century. The power of electricity had not yet been discovered and in the dark of night lit only by moonlight and stars the world took on an eerie and mysterious form. Scrooge was especially stingy and would light his room with only a single candle and out of that small light a ghost emerged, and ethereal being from another dimension with a message for Scrooge. What was this ghost like? It was gentle as it took Scrooge's arm gently. Yet later, when Scrooge tried to escape, the ghost pinned his arms determined that Scrooge would see the entire scene unfold wisely knowing that Scrooge must understand the entire circumstances that created the opportunity to make the choice of isolating himself to his only friend, money. Driven by the desire to make a change in Scrooge, the Ghost of Christmas Past knows that his determination will not only affect Scrooge but many people around him including his hired man Bob Cratchet, poor people whom he has thus far refused to help, and others. Most important, the ghost knows that he will help transform Scrooge into a bastion (stronghold) of society making his corner of the world a better place for many.

223 words

Meta Modal Challenge for this week is universal qualifiers. These include always, never, all, every, no one, everyone. They over generalize behaviors or relationships that have been seen to happen in a few instances to characterize all instances. To challenge the statement find a counterexample for the claim.

Children never got to play in the old days?

- Never? Were there some children who got to play in the old days?

This question is looking for the counter example of children who got to play in the old days.

A sample expansion to answer the question could be this sentence.

Young children had to work hard in many places in the old days in order to provide enough food to eat so they rarely had time to play.

Although poor children had little time for play in the old days, children from rich families often engaged in elaborate play with many toys such as wooden soldiers for the boys and dolls for the girls.

Lesson 15: A Christmas Carol and Outlines

Homework Assignment

Choose a topic to write you essay on. Go to the internet and find information about the topic of your choice. Make an outline. You must have four items of information about 19th century England and four items about your country today. Remember to choose a topic that will interest the reader. Remember to put the sources you used at the bottom of the outline.

Weekly Reading--A Christmas Carol

A CHRISTMAS CAROL

Stave 3

By Charles Dickens

Awaking in the middle of a prodigiously tough snore, and sitting up in bed to get his thoughts together, Scrooge had no occasion to be told that the bell was again upon the stroke of One. He felt that he was restored to consciousness in the right nick of time, for the especial purpose of holding a conference with the second messenger dispatched to him through Jacob Marley's intervention. But, finding that he turned uncomfortably cold when he began to wonder which of his curtains this new spectre would draw back, he put them every one aside with his own hands, and lying down again, established a sharp look-out all round the bed. For, he wished to challenge the Spirit on the moment of its appearance, and did not wish to be taken by surprise, and made nervous.

Gentlemen of the free-and-easy sort, who plume themselves on being acquainted with a move or two, and being usually equal to the time-of-day, express the wide range of their capacity for adventure by observing that they are good for anything from pitch-and-toss to manslaughter; between which opposite extremes, no doubt, there lies a tolerably wide and comprehensive range of subjects. Without venturing for Scrooge quite as hardily as this, I don't mind calling on you to believe that he was ready for a good broad field of strange appearances, and that nothing between a baby and rhinoceros would have astonished him very much.

Now, being prepared for almost anything, he was not by any means prepared for nothing; and, consequently, when the Bell struck One, and no shape appeared, he was taken with a violent fit of trembling. Five minutes, ten minutes, a quarter of an hour went by, yet nothing came. All this time, he lay upon his bed, the very core and centre of a blaze of ruddy light, which streamed upon it when the clock proclaimed the hour; and which, being only light, was more alarming than a dozen ghosts, as he was powerless to make out what it meant, or would be at; and was sometimes apprehensive that he might be at that very moment an interesting case of spontaneous combustion, without having the consolation of knowing it. At last, however, he began to think -- as you or I would have thought at first; for it is always the person not in the predicament who knows what ought to have been done in it, and would unquestionably have done it too -- at last, I say, he began to think that the source and secret of this ghostly light might be in the adjoining room, from whence, on further tracing it, it seemed to shine. This idea taking full possession of his mind, he got up softly and shuffled in his slippers to the door.

The moment Scrooge's hand was on the lock, a strange voice called him by his name, and bade him enter. He obeyed.

It was his own room. There was no doubt about that. But it had undergone a surprising transformation. The walls and ceiling were so hung with living green, that it looked a perfect grove; from every part of which, bright gleaming berries glistened. The crisp leaves of holly, mistletoe, and ivy reflected back the light, as if so many little mirrors had been scattered there; and such a mighty blaze went roaring up the chimney, as that dull petrifaction of a hearth had never known in Scrooge's time, or Marley's, or for many and many a winter season gone. Heaped up on the floor, to form a kind of throne, were turkeys, geese, game, poultry, brawn, great joints of meat, sucking-pigs, long wreaths of sausages, mince-pies, plum-puddings, barrels of oysters, red-hot chestnuts, cherry-cheeked apples, juicy oranges, luscious pears, immense twelfth-cakes, and seething bowls of punch, that made the chamber dim with their delicious steam. In easy state upon this couch, there sat a jolly Giant, glorious to see:, who bore a glowing torch, in shape not unlike Plenty's horn, and held it up, high up, to shed its light on Scrooge, as he came peeping round the door.

"Come in!" exclaimed the Ghost. "Come in, and know me better, man."

Scrooge entered timidly, and hung his head before this Spirit. He was not the dogged Scrooge he had been; and though the Spirit's eyes were clear and kind, he did not like to meet them.

"I am the Ghost of Christmas Present," said the Spirit. "Look upon me."

Scrooge reverently did so. It was clothed in one simple green robe, or mantle, bordered with white fur. This garment hung so loosely on the figure, that its capacious breast was bare, as if disdaining to be warded or concealed by any artifice. Its feet, observable beneath the ample folds of the garment, were also bare; and on its head it wore no other covering than a holly wreath, set here and there with shining icicles. Its dark brown curls were long and free; free as its genial face, its sparkling eye, its open hand, its cheery voice, its unconstrained demeanour, and its joyful air. Girded round its middle was an antique scabbard; but no sword was in it, and the ancient sheath was eaten up with rust.

"You have never seen the like of me before!" exclaimed the Spirit.

"Never," Scrooge made answer to it.

"Have never walked forth with the younger members of my family; meaning (for I am very young) my elder brothers born in these later years?" pursued the Phantom.

"I don't think I have," said Scrooge. "I am afraid I have not. Have you had many brothers, Spirit?"

"More than eighteen hundred," said the Ghost.

"A tremendous family to provide for," muttered Scrooge.

The Ghost of Christmas Present rose.

"Spirit," said Scrooge submissively, "conduct me where you will. I went forth last night on compulsion, and I learnt a lesson which is working now. To-night, if you have aught to teach me, let me profit by it."

"Touch my robe."

Scrooge did as he was told, and held it fast.

Holly, mistletoe, red berries, ivy, turkeys, geese, game, poultry, brawn, meat, pigs, sausages, oysters, pies, puddings, fruit, and punch, all vanished instantly. So did the room, the fire, the ruddy glow, the hour of night, and they stood in the city streets on Christmas morning, where (for the weather was severe) the people made a rough, but brisk and not unpleasant kind of music, in scraping the snow from the pavement in front of their dwellings, and from the tops of their houses, whence it was mad delight to the boys to see it come plumping down into the road below, and splitting into artificial little snow-storms.

The house fronts looked black enough, and the windows blacker, contrasting with the smooth white sheet of snow upon the roofs, and with the dirtier snow upon the ground; which last deposit had been ploughed up in deep furrows by the heavy wheels of carts and wagons; furrows that crossed and recrossed each other hundreds of times where the great streets branched off, and made intricate channels, hard to trace in the thick yellow mud and icy water. The sky was gloomy, and the shortest streets were choked up with a dingy mist, half thawed, half frozen, whose heavier particles descended in shower of sooty atoms, as if all the chimneys in Great Britain had, by one consent, caught fire, and were blazing away to their dear hearts" content. There was nothing very cheerful in the climate or the town, and yet was there an air of cheerfulness abroad that the clearest summer air and brightest summer sun might have endeavoured to diffuse in vain.

For, the people who were shovelling away on the housetops were jovial and full of glee; calling out to one another from the parapets, and now and then exchanging a facetious snowball -- better-natured missile far than many a wordy jest -- laughing heartily if it went right and not less heartily if it went wrong. The poulterers' shops were still half open, and the fruiterers' were radiant in their glory. There were great, round, pot-bellied baskets of chestnuts, shaped like the waistcoats of jolly old gentlemen, lolling at the doors, and tumbling out into the street in their apoplectic opulence. There were ruddy, brown-faced, broad-girthed Spanish Friars, and winking from their shelves in wanton slyness at the girls as they went by, and glanced demurely at the hung-up mistletoe. There were pears and apples, clustered high in blooming pyramids; there were bunches of grapes, made, in the shopkeepers" benevolence to dangle from conspicuous hooks, that people's mouths might water gratis as they passed; there were piles of filberts, mossy and brown, recalling, in their fragrance, ancient walks among the woods, and pleasant shufflings ankle deep through withered leaves; there were Norfolk Biffins, squab and swarthy, setting off the yellow of the oranges and lemons, and, in the great compactness of their juicy persons, urgently entreating and beseeching to be carried home in paper bags and eaten after dinner. The very gold and silver fish, set forth among these choice fruits in a bowl, though members of a dull and stagnant-blooded race, appeared to know that there was something going on; and, to a fish, went gasping round and round their little world in slow and passionless excitement.

The Grocers'! oh the Grocers'! Nearly closed, with perhaps two shutters down, or one; but through those gaps such glimpses. It was not alone that the scales descending on the counter made a merry sound, or that the twine and roller parted company so briskly, or that the canisters were rattled up and down like juggling tricks, or even that the blended scents of tea and coffee were so grateful to the nose, or even that the raisins were so plentiful and rare, the almonds so extremely white, the sticks of cinnamon so long and straight, the other spices so delicious, the candied fruits so caked and spotted with molten sugar as to make the coldest lookers-on feel faint and subsequently bilious. Nor was it that the figs were moist and pulpy, or that the French plums blushed in modest tartness from their highly-decorated boxes, or that everything was good to eat and in its Christmas dress; but the customers were all so hurried and so eager in the hopeful promise of the day, that they tumbled up against each other at the door, clashing their wicker baskets wildly, and left their purchases upon the counter, and came running back to fetch them, and committed hundreds of the like mistakes, in the best humour possible; while the Grocer and his people were so frank and fresh that the polished hearts with which they fastened their aprons behind might have been their own, worn outside for general inspection, and for Christmas daws to peck at if they chose.

But soon the steeples called good people all, to church and chapel, and away they came, flocking through the streets in their best clothes, and with their gayest faces. And at the same time there emerged from scores of bye-streets, lanes, and nameless turnings, innumerable people, carrying their dinners to the bakers' shops. The sight of these poor revellers appeared to interest the Spirit very much, for he stood with Scrooge beside him in a baker's doorway, and taking off the covers as their bearers passed, sprinkled incense on their dinners from his torch. And it was a very uncommon kind of torch, for once or twice when there were angry words between some dinner-carriers who had jostled each other, he shed a few drops of water on them from it, and their good humour was restored directly. For they said, it was a shame to quarrel upon Christmas Day. And so it was. God love it, so it was.

In time the bells ceased, and the bakers were shut up; and yet there was a genial shadowing forth of all these dinners and the progress of their cooking, in the thawed blotch of wet above each baker's oven; where the pavement smoked as if its stones were cooking too.

"Is there a peculiar flavour in what you sprinkle from your torch?" asked Scrooge.

"There is. My own."

"Would it apply to any kind of dinner on this day?" asked Scrooge.

"To any kindly given. To a poor one most."

"Why to a poor one most?" asked Scrooge.

"Because it needs it most."

"Spirit," said Scrooge, after a moment's thought, "I wonder you, of all the beings in the many worlds about us, should desire to cramp these people's opportunities of innocent enjoyment."

"I!" cried the Spirit.

"You would deprive them of their means of dining every seventh day, often the only day on which they can be said to dine at all," said Scrooge. "Wouldn't you?"

"I!" cried the Spirit.

"You seek to close these places on the Seventh Day," said Scrooge. "And it comes to the same thing."

"I seek!" exclaimed the Spirit.

"Forgive me if I am wrong. It has been done in your name, or at least in that of your family," said Scrooge.

"There are some upon this earth of yours," returned the Spirit, "who lay claim to know us, and who do their deeds of passion, pride, ill-will, hatred, envy, bigotry, and selfishness in our name, who are as strange to us and all our kith and kin, as if they had never lived. Remember that, and charge their doings on themselves, not us."

Scrooge promised that he would; and they went on, invisible, as they had been before, into the suburbs of the town. It was a remarkable quality of the Ghost (which Scrooge had observed at the baker's), that notwithstanding his gigantic size, he could accommodate himself to any place with ease; and that he stood beneath a low roof quite as gracefully and like a supernatural creature, as it was possible he could have done in any lofty hall.

And perhaps it was the pleasure the good Spirit had in showing off this power of his, or else it was his own kind, generous, hearty nature, and his sympathy with all poor men, that led him straight to Scrooge's clerk's; for there he went, and took Scrooge with him, holding to his robe; and on the threshold of the door the Spirit smiled, and stopped to bless Bob Cratchit's dwelling with the sprinkling of his torch. Think of that. Bob had but fifteen bob a-week himself; he pocketed on Saturdays but fifteen copies of his Christian name; and yet the Ghost of Christmas Present blessed his four-roomed house.

Then up rose Mr. s. Cratchit, Cratchit's wife, dressed out but poorly in a twice-turned gown, but brave in ribbons, which are cheap and make a goodly show for sixpence; and she laid the cloth, assisted by Belinda Cratchit, second of her daughters, also brave in ribbons; while Master Peter Cratchit plunged a fork into the saucepan of potatoes, and getting the corners of his monstrous shirt collar (Bob's private property, conferred upon his son and heir in honour of the day) into his mouth, rejoiced to find himself so gallantly attired, and yearned to show his linen in the fashionable Parks. And now two smaller Cratchits, boy and girl, came tearing in, screaming that outside the baker's they had smelt the goose, and known it for their own; and basking in luxurious thoughts of sage and onion, these young Cratchits danced about the table, and exalted Master Peter Cratchit to the skies, while he (not proud, although his collars nearly choked him) blew the fire, until the slow potatoes bubbling up, knocked loudly at the saucepan-lid to be let out and peeled.

"What has ever got your precious father then?" said Mr. s. Cratchit. "And your brother, Tiny Tim; And Martha warn't as late last Christmas Day by half-an-hour."

"Here's Martha, mother," said a girl, appearing as she spoke.

"Here's Martha, mother!" cried the two young Cratchits. "Hurrah! There's such a goose, Martha!"

"Why, bless your heart alive, my dear, how late you are!" said Mr. s. Cratchit, kissing her a dozen times, and taking off her shawl and bonnet for her with officious zeal.

"We'd a deal of work to finish up last night," replied the girl, "and had to clear away this morning, mother."

"Well. Never mind so long as you are come," said Mr. s. Cratchit. "Sit ye down before the fire, my dear, and have a warm, Lord bless ye."

"No, no. There's father coming," cried the two young Cratchits, who were everywhere at once. "Hide, Martha, hide!"

So Martha hid herself, and in came little Bob, the father, with at least three feet of comforter exclusive of the fringe, hanging down before him; and his threadbare clothes darned up and brushed, to look seasonable; and Tiny Tim upon his shoulder. Alas for Tiny Tim, he bore a little crutch, and had his limbs supported by an iron frame.

"Why, where's our Martha?" cried Bob Cratchit, looking round.

"Not coming," said Mr. s. Cratchit.

"Not coming!" said Bob, with a sudden declension in his high spirits; for he had been Tim's blood horse all the way from church, and had come home rampant. "Not coming upon Christmas Day?"

Martha didn't like to see him disappointed, if it were only in joke; so she came out prematurely from behind the closet door, and ran into his arms, while the two young Cratchits hustled Tiny Tim, and bore him off into the wash-house, that he might hear the pudding singing in the copper.

"And how did little Tim behave?" asked Mr. s. Cratchit, when she had rallied Bob on his credulity, and Bob had hugged his daughter to his heart's content.

"As good as gold," said Bob, "and better. Somehow he gets thoughtful sitting by himself so much, and thinks the strangest things you ever heard. He told me, coming home, that he hoped the people saw him in the church, because he was a cripple, and it might be pleasant to them to remember upon Christmas Day, who made lame beggars walk, and blind men see."

Bob's voice was tremulous when he told them this, and trembled more when he said that Tiny Tim was growing strong and hearty.

His active little crutch was heard upon the floor, and back came Tiny Tim before another word was spoken, escorted by his brother and sister to his stool before the fire; and while Bob, turning up his cuffs -- as if, poor fellow, they were capable of being made more shabby -- compounded some hot mixture in a jug with gin and lemons, and stirred it round and round and put it on the hob to simmer; Master Peter, and the two ubiquitous young Cratchits went to fetch the goose, with which they soon returned in high procession.

Such a bustle ensued that you might have thought a goose the rarest of all birds; a feathered phenomenon, to which a black swan was a matter of course -- and in truth it was something very like it in that house. Mr. s. Cratchit made the gravy (ready beforehand in a little saucepan) hissing hot; Master Peter mashed the potatoes with incredible vigour; Miss Belinda sweetened up the apple-sauce; Martha dusted the hot plates; Bob took Tiny Tim beside him in a tiny corner at the table; the two young Cratchits set chairs for everybody, not forgetting themselves, and mounting guard upon their posts, crammed spoons into their mouths, lest they should shriek for goose before their turn came to be helped. At last the dishes were set on, and grace was said. It was succeeded by a breathless pause, as Mr. s. Cratchit, looking slowly all along the carving-knife, prepared to plunge it in the breast; but when she did, and when the long expected gush of stuffing issued forth, one murmur of delight arose all round the board, and even Tiny Tim, excited by the two young Cratchits, beat on the table with the handle of his knife, and feebly cried Hurrah!

There never was such a goose. Bob said he didn't believe there ever was such a goose cooked. Its tenderness and flavour, size and cheapness, were the themes of universal admiration. Eked out by apple-sauce and mashed potatoes, it was a sufficient dinner for the whole family; indeed, as Mr. s. Cratchit said with great delight (surveying one small atom of a bone upon the dish), they hadn't ate it all at last. Yet every one had had enough, and the youngest Cratchits in particular, were steeped in sage and onion to the eyebrows. But now, the plates being changed by Miss Belinda, Mr. s. Cratchit left the room alone -- too nervous to bear witnesses -- to take the pudding up and bring it in.

Suppose it should not be done enough? Suppose it should break in turning out? Suppose somebody should have got over the wall of the back-yard, and stolen it, while they were merry with the goose -- a supposition at which the two young Cratchits became livid? All sorts of horrors were supposed.

Hallo! A great deal of steam! The pudding was out of the copper. A smell like a washing-day. That was the cloth. A smell like an eating-house and a pastrycook's next door to each other, with a laundress's next door to that. That was the pudding. In half a minute Mr. s. Cratchit entered -- flushed, but smiling proudly -- with the pudding, like a speckled cannon-ball, so hard and firm, blazing in half of half-a-quartern of ignited brandy, and bedight with Christmas holly stuck into the top.

Oh, a wonderful pudding! Bob Cratchit said, and calmly too, that he regarded it as the greatest success achieved by Mr. s. Cratchit since their marriage. Mr. s. Cratchit said that now the weight was off her mind, she would confess she had had her doubts about the quantity of flour. Everybody had something to say about it, but nobody said or thought it was at all a small pudding for a large family. It would have been flat heresy to do so. Any Cratchit would have blushed to hint at such a thing.

At last the dinner was all done, the cloth was cleared, the hearth swept, and the fire made up. The compound in the jug being tasted, and considered perfect, apples and oranges were put upon the table, and a shovel-full of chestnuts on the fire. Then all the Cratchit family drew round the hearth, in what Bob Cratchit called a circle, meaning half a one; and at Bob Cratchit's elbow stood the family display of glass. Two tumblers, and a custard-cup without a handle.

These held the hot stuff from the jug, however, as well as golden goblets would have done; and Bob served it out with beaming looks, while the chestnuts on the fire sputtered and cracked noisily. Then Bob proposed:

"A Merry Christmas to us all, my dears. God bless us."

Which all the family re-echoed.

"God bless us every one!" said Tiny Tim, the last of all.

He sat very close to his father's side upon his little stool. Bob held his withered little hand in his, as if he loved the child, and wished to keep him by his side, and dreaded that he might be taken from him.

"Spirit," said Scrooge, with an interest he had never felt before,"tell me if Tiny Tim will live."

"I see a vacant seat," replied the Ghost, "in the poor chimney-corner, and a crutch without an owner, carefully preserved. If these shadows remain unaltered by the Future, the child will die."

"No, no," said Scrooge. "Oh, no, kind Spirit. Say he will be spared."

"If these shadows remain unaltered by the Future, none other of my race," returned the Ghost, "will find him here. What then? If he be like to die, he had better do it, and decrease the surplus population."

Scrooge hung his head to hear his own words quoted by the Spirit, and was overcome with penitence and grief.

"Man," said the Ghost, "if man you be in heart, not adamant, forbear that wicked cant until you have discovered What the surplus is, and Where it is. Will you decide what men shall live, what men shall die? It may be, that in the sight of Heaven, you are more worthless and less fit to live than millions like this poor man's child. Oh God! To hear the Insect on the leaf pronouncing on the too much life among his hungry brothers in the dust."

Scrooge bent before the Ghost's rebuke, and trembling cast his eyes upon the ground. But he raised them speedily, on hearing his own name.

"Mr. Scrooge!" said Bob; "I'll give you Mr. Scrooge, the Founder of the Feast!"

"The Founder of the Feast indeed!" cried Mr. s. Cratchit, reddening. "I wish I had him here. I'd give him a piece of my mind to feast upon, and I hope he'd have a good appetite for it."

"My dear," said Bob, "the children. Christmas Day."

"It should be Christmas Day, I am sure," said she, "on which one drinks the health of such an odious, stingy, hard, unfeeling man as Mr. Scrooge. You know he is, Robert. Nobody knows it better than you do, poor fellow."

"My dear," was Bob's mild answer, "Christmas Day."

"I'll drink his health for your sake and the Day's," said Mr. s. Cratchit, "not for his. Long life to him. A merry Christmas and a happy new year! -- he'll be very merry and very happy, I have no doubt!"

The children drank the toast after her. It was the first of their proceedings which had no heartiness. Tiny Tim drank it last of all, but he didn't care twopence for it. Scrooge was the Ogre of the family. The mention of his name cast a dark shadow on the party, which was not dispelled for full five minutes.

After it had passed away, they were ten times merrier than before, from the mere relief of Scrooge the Baleful being done with. Bob Cratchit told them how he had a situation in his eye for Master Peter, which would bring in, if obtained, full five-and-sixpence weekly. The two young Cratchits laughed tremendously at the idea of Peter's being a man of business; and Peter himself looked thoughtfully at the fire from between his collars, as if he were deliberating what particular investments he should favour when he came into the receipt of that bewildering income. Martha, who was a poor apprentice at a milliner's, then told them what kind of work she had to do, and how many hours she worked at a stretch, and how she meant to lie abed to-morrow morning for a good long rest; to-morrow being a holiday she passed at home. Also how she had seen a countess and a lord some days before, and how the lord was much about as tall as Peter; at which Peter pulled up his collars so high that you couldn't have seen his head if you had been there. All this time the chestnuts and the jug went round and round; and by-and-bye they had a song, about a lost child travelling in the snow, from Tiny Tim, who had a plaintive little voice, and sang it very well indeed.

There was nothing of high mark in this. They were not a handsome family; they were not well dressed; their shoes were far from being water-proof; their clothes were scanty; and Peter might have known, and very likely did, the inside of a pawnbroker's. But, they were happy, grateful, pleased with one another, and contented with the time; and when they faded, and looked happier yet in the bright sprinklings of the Spirit's torch at parting, Scrooge had his eye upon them, and especially on Tiny Tim, until the last.

By this time it was getting dark, and snowing pretty heavily; and as Scrooge and the Spirit went along the streets, the brightness of the roaring fires in kitchens, parlours, and all sorts of rooms, was wonderful. Here, the flickering of the blaze showed preparations for a cosy dinner, with hot plates baking through and through before the fire, and deep red curtains, ready to be drawn to shut out cold and darkness. There all the children of the house were running out into the snow to meet their married sisters, brothers, cousins, uncles, aunts, and be the first to greet them. Here, again, were shadows on the window-blind of guests assembling; and there a group of handsome girls, all hooded and fur-booted, and all chattering at once, tripped lightly off to some near neighbour's house; where, woe upon the single man who saw them enter -- artful witches, well they knew it -- in a glow.

But, if you had judged from the numbers of people on their way to friendly gatherings, you might have thought that no one was at home to give them welcome when they got there, instead of every house expecting company, and piling up its fires half-chimney high. Blessings on it, how the Ghost exulted. How it bared its breadth of breast, and opened its capacious palm, and floated on, outpouring, with a generous hand, its bright and harmless mirth on everything within its reach. The very lamplighter, who ran on before dotting the dusky street with specks of light, and who was dressed to spend the evening somewhere, laughed out loudly as the Spirit passed, though little kenned the lamplighter that he had any company but Christmas.

And now, without a word of warning from the Ghost, they stood upon a bleak and desert moor, where monstrous masses of rude stone were cast about, as though it were the burial-place of giants; and water spread itself wheresoever it listed -- or would have done so, but for the frost that held it prisoner; and nothing grew but moss and furze, and coarse rank grass. Down in the west the setting sun had left a streak of fiery red, which glared upon the desolation for an instant, like a sullen eye, and frowning lower, lower, lower yet, was lost in the thick gloom of darkest night.

"What place is this?" asked Scrooge.

"A place where Miners live, who labour in the bowels of the earth," returned the Spirit. "But they know me. See."

A light shone from the window of a hut, and swiftly they advanced towards it. Passing through the wall of mud and stone, they found a cheerful company assembled round a glowing fire. An old, old man and woman, with their children and their children's children, and another generation beyond that, all decked out gaily in their holiday attire. The old man, in a voice that seldom rose above the howling of the wind upon the barren waste, was singing them a Christmas song -- it had been a very old song when he was a boy -- and from time to time they all joined in the chorus. So surely as they raised their voices, the old man got quite blithe and loud; and so surely as they stopped, his vigour sank again.

The Spirit did not tarry here, but bade Scrooge hold his robe, and passing on above the moor, sped -- whither. Not to sea? To sea. To Scrooge's horror, looking back, he saw the last of the land, a frightful range of rocks, behind them; and his ears were deafened by the thundering of water, as it rolled and roared, and raged among the dreadful caverns it had worn, and fiercely tried to undermine the earth.

Built upon a dismal reef of sunken rocks, some league or so from shore, on which the waters chafed and dashed, the wild year through, there stood a solitary lighthouse. Great heaps of sea-weed clung to its base, and storm-birds -- born of the wind one might suppose, as sea-weed of the water -- rose and fell about it, like the waves they skimmed.

But even here, two men who watched the light had made a fire, that through the loophole in the thick stone wall shed out a ray of brightness on the awful sea. Joining their horny hands over the rough table at which they sat, they wished each other Merry Christmas in their can of grog; and one of them: the elder, too, with his face all damaged and scarred with hard weather, as the figure-head of an old ship might be: struck up a sturdy song that was like a Gale in itself.

Again the Ghost sped on, above the black and heaving sea -- on, on -- until, being far away, as he told Scrooge, from any shore, they lighted on a ship. They stood beside the helmsman at the wheel, the look-out in the bow, the officers who had the watch; dark, ghostly figures in their several stations; but every man among them hummed a Christmas tune, or had a Christmas thought, or spoke below his breath to his companion of some bygone Christmas Day, with homeward hopes belonging to it. And every man on board, waking or sleeping, good or bad, had had a kinder word for another on that day than on any day in the year; and had shared to some extent in its festivities; and had remembered those he cared for at a distance, and had known that they delighted to remember him.

It was a great surprise to Scrooge, while listening to the moaning of the wind, and thinking what a solemn thing it was to move on through the lonely darkness over an unknown abyss, whose depths were secrets as profound as Death: it was a great surprise to Scrooge, while thus engaged, to hear a hearty laugh. It was a much greater surprise to Scrooge to recognise it as his own nephew's and to find himself in a bright, dry, gleaming room, with the Spirit standing smiling by his side, and looking at that same nephew with approving affability.

"Ha, ha!" laughed Scrooge's nephew. "Ha, ha, ha!"

If you should happen, by any unlikely chance, to know a man more blest in a laugh than Scrooge's nephew, all I can say is, I should like to know him too. Introduce him to me, and I'll cultivate his acquaintance.

It is a fair, even-handed, noble adjustment of things, that while there is infection in disease and sorrow, there is nothing in the world so irresistibly contagious as laughter and good-humour. When Scrooge's nephew laughed in this way: holding his sides, rolling his head, and twisting his face into the most extravagant contortions: Scrooge's niece, by marriage, laughed as heartily as he. And their assembled friends being not a bit behindhand, roared out lustily.

"Ha, ha! Ha, ha, ha, ha!"

"He said that Christmas was a humbug, as I live!" cried Scrooge's nephew. "He believed it too."

"More shame for him, Fred." said Scrooge's niece, indignantly. Bless those women; they never do anything by halves. They are always in earnest.

She was very pretty: exceedingly pretty. With a dimpled, surprised-looking, capital face; a ripe little mouth, that seemed made to be kissed -- as no doubt it was; all kinds of good little dots about her chin, that melted into one another when she laughed; and the sunniest pair of eyes you ever saw in any little creature's head. Altogether she was what you would have called provoking, you know; but satisfactory, too. Oh perfectly satisfactory!

"He's a comical old fellow," said Scrooge's nephew, "that's the truth: and not so pleasant as he might be. However, his offenses carry their own punishment, and I have nothing to say against him."

"I'm sure he is very rich, Fred," hinted Scrooge's niece. "At least you always tell me so."

"What of that, my dear?" said Scrooge's nephew. "His wealth is of no use to him. He don't do any good with it. He don't make himself comfortable with it. He hasn't the satisfaction of thinking -- ha, ha, ha! -- that he is ever going to benefit us with it."

"I have no patience with him," observed Scrooge's niece. Scrooge's niece's sisters, and all the other ladies, expressed the same opinion.

"Oh, I have," said Scrooge's nephew. "I am sorry for him; I couldn't be angry with him if I tried. Who suffers by his ill whims? Himself, always. Here, he takes it into his head to dislike us, and he won't come and dine with us. What's the consequence? He don't lose much of a dinner."

"Indeed, I think he loses a very good dinner," interrupted Scrooge's niece. Everybody else said the same, and they must be allowed to have been competent judges, because they had just had dinner; and, with the dessert upon the table, were clustered round the fire, by lamplight.

"Well. I'm very glad to hear it," said Scrooge's nephew, "because I haven't great faith in these young housekeepers. What do you say, Topper?"

Topper had clearly got his eye upon one of Scrooge's niece's sisters, for he answered that a bachelor was a wretched outcast, who had no right to express an opinion on the subject. Whereat Scrooge's niece's sister -- the plump one with the lace tucker: not the one with the roses -- blushed.

"Do go on, Fred," said Scrooge's niece, clapping her hands. "He never finishes what he begins to say. He is such a ridiculous fellow."

Scrooge's nephew revelled in another laugh, and as it was impossible to keep the infection off; though the plump sister tried hard to do it with aromatic vinegar; his example was unanimously followed.

"I was only going to say," said Scrooge's nephew," that the consequence of his taking a dislike to us, and not making merry with us, is, as I think, that he loses some pleasant moments, which could do him no harm. I am sure he loses pleasanter companions than he can find in his own thoughts, either in his mouldy old office, or his dusty chambers. I mean to give him the same chance every year, whether he likes it or not, for I pity him. He may rail at Christmas till he dies, but he can't help thinking better of it -- I defy him -- if he finds me going there, in good temper, year after year, and saying Uncle Scrooge, how are you. If it only puts him in the vein to leave his poor clerk fifty pounds, that's something; and I think I shook him yesterday."

It was their turn to laugh now at the notion of his shaking Scrooge. But being thoroughly good-natured, and not much caring what they laughed at, so that they laughed at any rate, he encouraged them in their merriment, and passed the bottle joyously.

After tea they had some music. For they were a musical family, and knew what they were about, when they sung a Glee or Catch, I can assure you: especially Topper, who could growl away in the bass like a good one, and never swell the large veins in his forehead, or get red in the face over it. Scrooge's niece played well upon the harp; and played among other tunes a simple little air (a mere nothing: you might learn to whistle it in two minutes), which had been familiar to the child who fetched Scrooge from the boarding-school, as he had been reminded by the Ghost of Christmas Past. When this strain of music sounded, all the things that Ghost had shown him, came upon his mind; he softened more and more; and thought that if he could have listened to it often, years ago, he might have cultivated the kindnesses of life for his own happiness with his own hands, without resorting to the sexton's spade that buried Jacob Marley.

But they didn't devote the whole evening to music. After a while they played at forfeits; for it is good to be children sometimes, and never better than at Christmas, when its mighty Founder was a child himself. Stop. There was first a game at blind-man's buff. Of course there was. And I no more believe Topper was really blind than I believe he had eyes in his boots. My opinion is, that it was a done thing between him and Scrooge's nephew; and that the Ghost of Christmas Present knew it. The way he went after that plump sister in the lace tucker, was an outrage on the credulity of human nature. Knocking down the fire-irons, tumbling over the chairs, bumping against the piano, smothering himself among the curtains, wherever she went, there went he. He always knew where the plump sister was. He wouldn't catch anybody else. If you had fallen up against him (as some of them did), on purpose, he would have made a feint of endeavouring to seize you, which would have been an affront to your understanding, and would instantly have sidled off in the direction of the plump sister. She often cried out that it wasn't fair; and it really was not. But when at last, he caught her; when, in spite of all her silken rustlings, and her rapid flutterings past him, he got her into a corner whence there was no escape; then his conduct was the most execrable. For his pretending not to know her; his pretending that it was necessary to touch her head-dress, and further to assure himself of her identity by pressing a certain ring upon her finger, and a certain chain about her neck; was vile, monstrous. No doubt she told him her opinion of it, when, another blind-man being in office, they were so very confidential together, behind the curtains.

Scrooge's niece was not one of the blind-man's buff party, but was made comfortable with a large chair and a footstool, in a snug corner, where the Ghost and Scrooge were close behind her. But she joined in the forfeits, and loved her love to admiration with all the letters of the alphabet. Likewise at the game of How, When, and Where, she was very great, and to the secret joy of Scrooge's nephew, beat her sisters hollow: though they were sharp girls too, as could have told you. There might have been twenty people there, young and old, but they all played, and so did Scrooge, for, wholly forgetting the interest he had in what was going on, that his voice made no sound in their ears, he sometimes came out with his guess quite loud, and very often guessed quite right, too; for the sharpest needle, best Whitechapel, warranted not to cut in the eye, was not sharper than Scrooge; blunt as he took it in his head to be.

The Ghost was greatly pleased to find him in this mood, and looked upon him with such favour, that he begged like a boy to be allowed to stay until the guests departed. But this the Spirit said could not be done.

"Here's a new game," said Scrooge. "One half hour, Spirit, only one."

It was a Game called Yes and No, where Scrooge's nephew had to think of something, and the rest must find out what; he only answering to their questions yes or no, as the case was. The brisk fire of questioning to which he was exposed, elicited from him that he was thinking of an animal, a live animal, rather a disagreeable animal, a savage animal, an animal that growled and grunted sometimes, and talked sometimes, and lived in London, and walked about the streets, and wasn't made a show of, and wasn't led by anybody, and didn't live in a menagerie, and was never killed in a market, and was not a horse, or an ass, or a cow, or a bull, or a tiger, or a dog, or a pig, or a cat, or a bear. At every fresh question that was put to him, this nephew burst into a fresh roar of laughter; and was so inexpressibly tickled, that he was obliged to get up off the sofa and stamp. At last the plump sister, falling into a similar state, cried out:

"I have found it out! I know what it is, Fred! I know what it is!"

"What is it?" cried Fred.

"It's your Uncle Scrooge!"

Which it certainly was. Admiration was the universal sentiment, though some objected that the reply to "Is it a bear?" ought to have been "Yes," inasmuch as an answer in the negative was sufficient to have diverted their thoughts from Mr. Scrooge, supposing they had ever had any tendency that way.

"He has given us plenty of merriment, I am sure," said Fred, "and it would be ungrateful not to drink his health. Here is a glass of mulled wine ready to our hand at the moment; and I say, " 'Uncle Scrooge!' "

"Well! Uncle Scrooge!" they cried.

"A Merry Christmas and a Happy New Year to the old man, whatever he is," said Scrooge's nephew. "He wouldn't take it from me, but may he have it, nevertheless. Uncle Scrooge!"

Uncle Scrooge had imperceptibly become so gay and light of heart, that he would have pledged the unconscious company in return, and thanked them in an inaudible speech, if the Ghost had given him time. But the whole scene passed off in the breath of the last word spoken by his nephew; and he and the Spirit were again upon their travels.

Much they saw, and far they went, and many homes they visited, but always with a happy end. The Spirit stood beside sick beds, and they were cheerful; on foreign lands, and they were close at home; by struggling men, and they were patient in their greater hope; by poverty, and it was rich. In almshouse, hospital, and jail, in misery's every refuge, where vain man in his little brief authority had not made fast the door and barred the Spirit out, he left his blessing, and taught Scrooge his precepts.

It was a long night, if it were only a night; but Scrooge had his doubts of this, because the Christmas Holidays appeared to be condensed into the space of time they passed together. It was strange, too, that while Scrooge remained unaltered in his outward form, the Ghost grew older, clearly older. Scrooge had observed this change, but never spoke of it, until they left a children's Twelfth Night party, when, looking at the Spirit as they stood together in an open place, he noticed that its hair was grey.

"Are spirits' lives so short?" asked Scrooge.

"My life upon this globe, is very brief," replied the Ghost. "It ends to-night."

"To-night!" cried Scrooge.

"To-night at midnight. Hark! The time is drawing near."

The chimes were ringing the three quarters past eleven at that moment.

"Forgive me if I am not justified in what I ask," said Scrooge, looking intently at the Spirit's robe, "but I see something strange, and not belonging to yourself, protruding from your skirts. Is it a foot or a claw?"

"It might be a claw, for the flesh there is upon it," was the Spirit's sorrowful reply. "Look here."

From the foldings of its robe, it brought two children; wretched, abject, frightful, hideous, miserable. They knelt down at its feet, and clung upon the outside of its garment.

"Oh, Man, look here! Look, look, down here!" exclaimed the Ghost.

They were a boy and a girl. Yellow, meagre, ragged, scowling, wolfish; but prostrate, too, in their humility. Where graceful youth should have filled their features out, and touched them with its freshest tints, a stale and shrivelled hand, like that of age, had pinched, and twisted them, and pulled them into shreds. Where angels might have sat enthroned, devils lurked, and glared out menacing. No change, no degradation, no perversion of humanity, in any grade, through all the mysteries of wonderful creation, has monsters half so horrible and dread.

Scrooge started back, appalled. Having them shown to him in this way, he tried to say they were fine children, but the words choked themselves, rather than be parties to a lie of such enormous magnitude.

"Spirit, are they yours?" Scrooge could say no more.

"They are Man's," said the Spirit, looking down upon them. "And they cling to me, appealing from their fathers. This boy is Ignorance. This girl is Want. Beware them both, and all of their degree, but most of all beware this boy, for on his brow I see that written which is Doom, unless the writing be erased. Deny it!" cried the Spirit, stretching out its hand towards the city. "Slander those who tell it ye. Admit it for your factious purposes, and make it worse. And abide the end."

"Have they no refuge or resource?" cried Scrooge.

"Are there no prisons?" said the Spirit, turning on him for the last time with his own words. "Are there no workhouses?"

The bell struck twelve.

Scrooge looked about him for the Ghost, and saw it not. As the last stroke ceased to vibrate, he remembered the prediction of old Jacob Marley, and lifting up his eyes, beheld a solemn Phantom, draped and hooded, coming, like a mist along the ground, towards him.

Making an Outline

Your assignment is to create an outline for your essay that you will start next week.

The essay is *Compare and Contrast 19th Century England with Your Country Today*.

The topic is too broad (big). You need to narrow it down. Think of what you might be interested in. Are you interested in clothes, commerce, government systems, food, or treatment of the handicapped? Maybe there is something else. You choose an area to share. It must fit under the topic "Compare and Contrast 19th Century England with China Today."

Then go to the internet. You will need at least 2 sources to go to. Gather information from these sources and put them into your graphic organizer. You must have at least eight pieces of information. You may have more. Wikipedia is a quick source of information but it is not always accurate. You will need two sources for this assignment. Only one can be Wikipedia.

When you are done, hand it in. You will then use that outline to help you write your essay in the upcoming lesson.

Here is an outline that is simple and fills the requirements. Note the topic is narrowed down well.

Compare and Contrast Men's Pants
in 19th Century England and China Today

long title. All important words in upper case
skip a space between title and first entry

I. England 19th century *use Roman numerals* I. II. III. IV.
   A. Home made there is a period after every number and letter. Then two spaces
   B. Wool, linen or cotton the first word is always capitalized
   C. From waist to ankle *Unless the teacher requires sentences, words or phrases are all you need*
   D. Button fly
   skip a space here before you put Roman Numeral II.

II. China
   A. Factory made
   B. Often denim jeans
      1. Of cotton
      2. Cotton blend
   C. Waist to ankle
   D. Zipper fly

The western outline follows a very particular form. Use the following form to help you organize our information.

Title			
I.	19th Century England		
	A.		
		1.	
		2.	
		3.	
		4.	
II.	China (USA, Korea etc. Whatever country you are from)		
	B.		
		1.	
		2.	
		3.	
		4.	

Sources:	
1.	
2.	

Remember to remove the lines before you print it.

Sample

Here are steps to follow. First get decide what you want to talk on and put it in the title. Make sure you capitalize every important word in the title and the first and last words.

This is a much more advanced outline, far more advanced that you need for this assignment. It shows you how an outline works.

Comparing Dance in 19th Century England with Dance in the USA Today			
I.	Dance in 19th Century England		
	A.	Dance steps	
		1.	Very stylized
		2.	Steps came from Irish Jigs
		3.	Steps came from France Waltzes
		4.	Steps were complicated
	B.	Dance costumes	
		1.	Costumes were heavy
		2.	Costumes were made of wool or cotton
		3.	Costumes were highly embroidered
		4.	Costumes usually covered the whole body
	C.	Dance Performance	
		1.	Performances were often on stage
		2.	Dancers were highly trained
		3.	Men and women were usually partners

II.	Dance in China today		
	A.	Dance steps	
		1.	Dances steps are taking from all over the world
		2.	Dances are learned from the internet
		3.	Dances are often complicated
		4.	Dances patterns are usually not stylized
	B.	Dance costumes	
		1.	Dancers often wear street clothes
		2.	Costumes are light and airy
		3.	Costumes designs come from all over the world
		4.	Costumes are often made of silk or imitation silk
	C.	Dance Performance	
		1.	Dancers often perform on stages
		2.	Dancers dance in parks and quiet streets
		3.	Dancers may do pageants with other groups
		4.	Dancers may perform on sport fields

Next put the information you found on the internet into the format. You can make it longer if you like.

Note that there are no periods at the end of each phrase. The outline is made from words and phrases, not complete sentences.

Remember you must have at least eight pieces of information. You may put in more if you like. I put in a lot more. It is a subject I am familiar with and know a lot about. If you choose a subject you are interested in you will have a lot also.

Now add sources. Use at least two. Only one can be Wikipedia.

Sources:

http://www.memory.loc.gov/ammem/dihtml/diessay6.html

http://en.wikipedia.org/wiki/Dance_in_China

You might also want to add pictures that you could use in your final essay.

One more step. Take out the lines. Highlight the entire section. Go to borders and click no borders. It is on the home page.

Make certain your name and student number are on the document and print it out to bring to class next week.

name	Prof. R.
Number	1234567890
	Lesson 12

Comparing Dance in 19th Century England with Dance in the USA Today

I. Dance in 19th Century England
   A. Dance steps
      1. Very stylized
      2. Steps came from Irish Jigs
      3. Steps came from France Waltzes
      4. Steps were complicated

B. Dance costumes
   1. Costumes were heavy
   2. Costumes were made of wool or cotton
   3. Costumes were highly embroidered
   4. Costumes usually covered the whole body
C. Dance Performance
   1. Performances were often on stage
   2. Dancers were highly trained
   3. Men and women were usually partners

II. Dance in China today
   A. Dance steps
      1. Dances steps are taking from all over the world
      2. Dances are learned from the internet
      3. Dances are often complicated
      4. Dances patterns are usually not stylized
   B. Dance costumes
      1. Dancers often wear street clothes
      2. Costumes are light and airy
      3. Costumes designs come from all over the world
      4. Costumes are often made of silk or imitation silk
   C. Dance Performance
      1. Dancers often perform on stages
      2. Dancers dance in parks and quiet streets
      3. Dancers may do pageants with other groups
      4. Dancers may perform on sport fields

Sources:
http://www.memory.loc.gov/ammem/dihtml/diessay6.html
http://en.wikipedia.org/wiki/Dance_in_China

Meta Model Challenge

Our challenge for this lesson is Model Operators of Possibility. These are words such as can't, impossible, won't, couldn't,

- It can't possibly be Tiny Tim?

Why can't it be, I hear Tiny Tim has found a doctor who can heal him and he is walking around Shanghai on holiday.

Lesson 16: A Christmas Carol and Compare and Contrast Essays

Homework Assignment

Using your outline, write a three paragraph compare and contrast paper on the subject that you have chosen to compare from 19th Century England compared to your country today. Remember to give it a title and put a space between your title and your essay. Print out your essay and bring it to class next week. We will peer edit the essays and your final essay will be due the week after that.

Weekly Reading--A Christmas Carol

Stave 4: The Last of the Spirits

The Phantom slowly, gravely, silently approached. When it came, Scrooge bent down upon his knee; for in the very air through which this Spirit moved it seemed to scatter gloom and mystery.

It was shrouded in a deep black garment, which concealed its head, its face, its form, and left nothing of it visible save one outstretched hand. But for this it would have been difficult to detach its figure from the night, and separate it from the darkness by which it was surrounded.

He felt that it was tall and stately when it came beside him, and that its mysterious presence filled him with a solemn dread. He knew no more, for the Spirit neither spoke nor moved.

"I am in the presence of the Ghost of Christmas Yet To Come?" said Scrooge.

The Spirit answered not, but pointed downward with its hand.

"You are about to show me shadows of the things that have not happened, but will happen in the time before us," Scrooge pursued. "Is that so, Spirit?"

The upper portion of the garment was contracted for an instant in its folds, as if the Spirit had inclined its head. That was the only answer he received.

Although well used to ghostly company by this time, Scrooge feared the silent shape so much that his legs trembled beneath him, and he found that he could hardly stand when he prepared to follow it. The Spirit pauses a moment, as observing his condition, and giving him time to recover.

But Scrooge was all the worse for this. It thrilled him with a vague uncertain horror, to know that behind the dusky shroud there were ghostly eyes intently fixed upon him, while he, though he stretched his own to the utmost, could see nothing but a spectral hand and one great heap of black.

"Ghost of the Future!" he exclaimed, "I fear you more than any spectre I have seen. But as I know your purpose is to do me good, and as I hope to live to be another man from what I was, I am prepared to bear you company, and do it with a thankful heart. Will you not speak to me?"

It gave him no reply. The hand was pointed straight before them.

"Lead on," said Scrooge. "Lead on. The night is waning fast, and it is precious time to me, I know. Lead on, Spirit."

The Phantom moved away as it had come towards him. Scrooge followed in the shadow of its dress, which bore him up, he thought, and carried him along.

They scarcely seemed to enter the city; for the city rather seemed to spring up about them, and encompass them of its own act. But there they were, in the heart of it; on Change, amongst the merchants; who hurried up and down, and chinked the money in their pockets, and conversed in groups, and looked at their watches, and trifled thoughtfully with their great gold seals; and so forth, as Scrooge had seen them often.

The Spirit stopped beside one little knot of business men. Observing that the hand was pointed to them, Scrooge advanced to listen to their talk.

"No," said a great fat man with a monstrous chin," I don't know much about it, either way. I only know he's dead."

"When did he die?" inquired another.

"Last night, I believe."

"Why, what was the matter with him?" asked a third, taking a vast quantity of snuff out of a very large snuff-box. "I thought he'd never die."

"God knows," said the first, with a yawn.

"What has he done with his money?" asked a red-faced gentleman with a pendulous excrescence on the end of his nose, that shook like the gills of a turkey-cock.

"I haven't heard," said the man with the large chin, yawning again. "Left it to his company, perhaps. He hasn't left it to me. That's all I know."

This pleasantry was received with a general laugh.

"It's likely to be a very cheap funeral," said the same speaker; "for upon my life I don't know of anybody to go to it. Suppose we make up a party and volunteer?"

"I don't mind going if a lunch is provided," observed the gentleman with the excrescence on his nose. "But I must be fed, if I make one."

Another laugh.

"Well, I am the most disinterested among you, after all," said the first speaker," for I never wear black gloves, and I never eat lunch. But I'll offer to go, if anybody else will. When I come to think of it, I'm not at all sure that I wasn't his most particular friend; for we used to stop and speak whenever we met. Bye, bye."

Speakers and listeners strolled away, and mixed with other groups. Scrooge knew the men, and looked towards the Spirit for an explanation.

The Phantom glided on into a street. Its finger pointed to two persons meeting. Scrooge listened again, thinking that the explanation might lie here.

He knew these men, also, perfectly. They were men of aye business: very wealthy, and of great importance. He had made a point always of standing well in their esteem: in a business point of view, that is; strictly in a business point of view.

"How are you?" said one.

"How are you?" returned the other.

"Well!" said the first. "Old Scratch has got his own at last, hey."

"So I am told," returned the second. "Cold, isn't it."

"Seasonable for Christmas time. You're not a skater, I suppose?"

"No. No. Something else to think of. Good morning."

Not another word. That was their meeting, their conversation, and their parting.

Scrooge was at first inclined to be surprised that the Spirit should attach importance to conversations apparently so trivial; but feeling assured that they must have some hidden purpose, he set himself to consider what it was likely to be. They could scarcely be supposed to have any bearing on the death of Jacob, his old partner, for that was Past, and this Ghost's province was the Future. Nor could he think of any one immediately connected with himself, to whom he could apply them. But nothing doubting that to whomsoever they applied they had some latent moral for his own improvement, he resolved to treasure up every word he heard, and everything he saw; and especially to observe the shadow of himself when it appeared. For he had an expectation that the conduct of his future self would give him the clue he missed, and would render the solution of these riddles easy.

He looked about in that very place for his own image; but another man stood in his accustomed corner, and though the clock pointed to his usual time of day for being there, he saw no likeness of himself among the multitudes that poured in through the Porch. It gave him little surprise, however; for he had been revolving in his mind a change of life, and thought and hoped he saw his new-born resolutions carried out in this.

Quiet and dark, beside him stood the Phantom, with its outstretched hand. When he roused himself from his thoughtful quest, he fancied from the turn of the hand, and its situation in reference to himself, that the Unseen Eyes were looking at him keenly. It made him shudder, and feel very cold.

They left the busy scene, and went into an obscure part of the town, where Scrooge had never penetrated before, although he recognised its situation, and its bad repute. The ways were foul and narrow; the shops and houses wretched; the people half-naked, drunken, slipshod, ugly. Alleys and archways, like so many cesspools, disgorged their offenses of smell, and dirt, and life, upon the straggling streets; and the whole quarter reeked with crime, with filth, and misery.

Far in this den of infamous resort, there was a low-browed, beetling shop, below a pent-house roof, where iron, old rags, bottles, bones, and greasy offal, were bought. Upon the floor within, were piled up heaps of rusty keys, nails, chains, hinges, files, scales, weights, and refuse iron of all kinds. Secrets that few would like to scrutinise were bred and hidden in mountains of unseemly rags, masses of corrupted fat, and sepulchres of bones. Sitting in among the wares he dealt in, by a charcoal stove, made of old bricks, was a grey-haired rascal, nearly seventy years of age; who had screened himself from the cold air without, by a frowsy curtaining of miscellaneous tatters, hung upon a line; and smoked his pipe in all the luxury of calm retirement.

Scrooge and the Phantom came into the presence of this man, just as a woman with a heavy bundle slunk into the shop. But she had scarcely entered, when another woman, similarly laden, came in too; and she was closely followed by a man in faded black, who was no less startled by the sight of them, than they had been upon the recognition of each other. After a short period of blank astonishment, in which the old man with the pipe had joined them, they all three burst into a laugh.

"Let the charwoman alone to be the first!" cried she who had entered first. "Let the laundress alone to be the second; and let the undertaker's man alone to be the third. Look here, old Joe, here's a chance. If we haven't all three met here without meaning it!"

"You couldn't have met in a better place," said old Joe, removing his pipe from his mouth. "Come into the parlour. You were made free of it long ago, you know; and the other two an't strangers. Stop till I shut the door of the shop. Ah. How it skreeks. There an't such a rusty bit of metal in the place as its own hinges, I believe; and I'm sure there's no such old bones here, as mine. Ha, ha! We're all suitable to our calling, we're well matched. Come into the parlour. Come into the parlour."

The parlour was the space behind the screen of rags. The old man raked the fire together with an old stair-rod, and having trimmed his smoky lamp (for it was night), with the stem of his pipe, put it in his mouth again.

While he did this, the woman who had already spoken threw her bundle on the floor, and sat down in a flaunting manner on a stool; crossing her elbows on her knees, and looking with a bold defiance at the other two.

"What odds then. What odds, Mr. Dilber ." said the woman. "Every person has a right to take care of themselves. He always did."

"That's true, indeed," said the laundress. "No man more so."

"Why then, don't stand staring as if you was afraid, woman; who's the wiser? We're not going to pick holes in each other's coats, I suppose?"

"No, indeed," said Mr. Dilber and the man together. "We should hope not."

"Very well, then!" cried the woman. "That's enough. Who's the worse for the loss of a few things like these? Not a dead man, I suppose."

"No, indeed," said Mr. Dilber, laughing.

"If he wanted to keep them after he was dead, a wicked old screw," pursued the woman, "why wasn't he natural in his lifetime? If he had been, he'd have had somebody to look after him when he was struck with Death, instead of lying gasping out his last there, alone by himself."

"It's the truest word that ever was spoke," said Mr. Dilber. "It's a judgment on him."

"I wish it was a little heavier judgment," replied the woman; "and it should have been, you may depend upon it, if I could have laid my hands on anything else. Open that bundle, old Joe, and let me know the value of it. Speak out plain. I'm not afraid to be the first, nor afraid for them to see it. We know pretty well that we were helping ourselves, before we met here, I believe. It's no sin. Open the bundle, Joe."

But the gallantry of her friends would not allow of this; and the man in faded black, mounting the breach first, produced his plunder. It was not extensive. A seal or two, a pencil-case, a pair of sleeve-buttons, and a brooch of no great value, were all. They were severally examined and appraised by old Joe, who chalked the sums he was disposed to give for each upon the wall, and added them up into a total when he found there was nothing more to come.

"That's your account," said Joe, "and I wouldn't give another sixpence, if I was to be boiled for not doing it. Who's next?"

Mr. Dilber was next. Sheets and towels, a little wearing apparel, two old-fashioned silver teaspoons, a pair of sugar-tongs, and a few boots. Her account was stated on the wall in the same manner.

"I always give too much to ladies. It's a weakness of mine, and that's the way I ruin myself," said old Joe. "That's your account. If you asked me for another penny, and made it an open question, I'd repent of being so liberal and knock off half-a-crown."

"And now undo my bundle, Joe," said the first woman.

Joe went down on his knees for the greater convenience of opening it, and having unfastened a great many knots, dragged out a large and heavy roll of some dark stuff.

"What do you call this?" said Joe. "Bed-curtains?"

"Ah!" returned the woman, laughing and leaning forward on her crossed arms. "Bed-curtains."

"You don't mean to say you took them down, rings and all, with him lying there?" said Joe.

"Yes I do," replied the woman. "Why not?"

"You were born to make your fortune," said Joe," and you'll certainly do it."

"I certainly shan't hold my hand, when I can get anything in it by reaching it out, for the sake of such a man as he was, I promise you, Joe," returned the woman coolly. "Don't drop that oil upon the blankets, now."

"His blankets?" asked Joe.

"Whose else's do you think?" replied the woman. "He isn't likely to take cold without them, I dare say."

"I hope he didn't die of any thing catching. Eh?" said old Joe, stopping in his work, and looking up.

"Don't you be afraid of that," returned the woman. "I an't so fond of his company that I'd loiter about him for such things, if he did. Ah. you may look through that shirt till your eyes ache; but you won't find a hole in it, nor a threadbare place. It's the best he had, and a fine one too. They'd have wasted it, if it hadn't been for me."

"What do you call wasting of it?" asked old Joe.

"Putting it on him to be buried in, to be sure," replied the woman with a laugh. "Somebody was fool enough to do it, but I took it off again. If calico an't good enough for such a purpose, it isn't good enough for anything. It's quite as becoming to the body. He can't look uglier than he did in that one."

Scrooge listened to this dialogue in horror. As they sat grouped about their spoil, in the scanty light afforded by the old man's lamp, he viewed them with a detestation and disgust, which could hardly have been greater, though they demons, marketing the corpse itself.

"Ha, ha!" laughed the same woman, when old Joe, producing a flannel bag with money in it, told out their several gains upon the ground. "This is the end of it, you see. He frightened every one away from him when he was alive, to profit us when he was dead. Ha, ha, ha!"

"Spirit," said Scrooge, shuddering from head to foot. "I see, I see. The case of this unhappy man might be my own. My life tends that way, now. Merciful Heaven, what is this?"

He recoiled in terror, for the scene had changed, and now he almost touched a bed: a bare, uncurtained bed: on which, beneath a ragged sheet, there lay a something covered up, which, though it was dumb, announced itself in awful language.

The room was very dark, too dark to be observed with any accuracy, though Scrooge glanced round it in obedience to a secret impulse, anxious to know what kind of room it was. A pale light, rising in the outer air, fell straight upon the bed; and on it, plundered and bereft, unwatched, unwept, uncared for, was the body of this man.

Scrooge glanced towards the Phantom. Its steady hand was pointed to the head. The cover was so carelessly adjusted that the slightest raising of it, the motion of a finger upon Scrooge's part, would have disclosed the face. He thought of it, felt how easy it would be to do, and longed to do it; but had no more power to withdraw the veil than to dismiss the spectre at his side.

Oh cold, cold, rigid, dreadful Death, set up thine altar here, and dress it with such terrors as thou hast at thy command: for this is thy dominion. But of the loved, revered, and honoured head, thou canst not turn one hair to thy dread purposes, or make one feature odious. It is not that the hand is heavy and will fall down when released; it is not that the heart and pulse are still; but that the hand was open, generous, and true; the heart brave, warm, and tender; and the pulse a man's. Strike, Shadow, strike. And see his good deeds springing from the wound, to sow the world with life immortal!

No voice pronounced these words in Scrooge's ears, and yet he heard them when he looked upon the bed. He thought, if this man could be raised up now, what would be his foremost thoughts. Avarice, hard-dealing, griping cares. They have brought him to a rich end, truly.

He lay, in the dark empty house, with not a man, a woman, or a child, to say that he was kind to me in this or that, and for the memory of one kind word I will be kind to him. A cat was tearing at the door, and there was a sound of gnawing rats beneath the hearth-stone. What they wanted in the room of death, and why they were so restless and disturbed, Scrooge did not dare to think.

"Spirit,." he said, "this is a fearful place. In leaving it, I shall not leave its lesson, trust me. Let us go."

Still the Ghost pointed with an unmoved finger to the head.

"I understand you," Scrooge returned, "and I would do it, if I could. But I have not the power, Spirit. I have not the power."

Again it seemed to look upon him.

"If there is any person in the town, who feels emotion caused by this man's death," said Scrooge quite agonised, "show that person to me, Spirit, I beseech you."

The Phantom spread its dark robe before him for a moment, like a wing; and withdrawing it, revealed a room by daylight, where a mother and her children were.

She was expecting some one, and with anxious eagerness; for she walked up and down the room; started at every sound; looked out from the window; glanced at the clock; tried, but in vain, to work with her needle; and could hardly bear the voices of the children in their play.

At length the long-expected knock was heard. She hurried to the door, and met her husband; a man whose face was careworn and depressed, though he was young. There was a remarkable expression in it now; a kind of serious delight of which he felt ashamed, and which he struggled to repress.

He sat down to the dinner that had been boarding for him by the fire; and when she asked him faintly what news (which was not until after a long silence), he appeared embarrassed how to answer.

"Is it good." she said, "or bad?" -- to help him.

"Bad," he answered.

"We are quite ruined."

"No. There is hope yet, Caroline."

"If he relents," she said, amazed, "there is. Nothing is past hope, if such a miracle has happened."

"He is past relenting," said her husband. "He is dead."

She was a mild and patient creature if her face spoke truth; but she was thankful in her soul to hear it, and she said so, with clasped hands. She prayed forgiveness the next moment, and was sorry; but the first was the emotion of her heart.

"What the half-drunken woman whom I told you of last night, said to me, when I tried to see him and obtain a week's delay; and what I thought was a mere excuse to avoid me; turns out to have been quite true. He was not only very ill, but dying, then."

"To whom will our debt be transferred?"

"I don't know. But before that time we shall be ready with the money; and even though we were not, it would be a bad fortune indeed to find so merciless a creditor in his successor. We may sleep to-night with light hearts, Caroline."

Yes. Soften it as they would, their hearts were lighter. The children's faces hushed, and clustered round to hear what they so little understood, were brighter; and it was a happier house for this man's death. The only emotion that the Ghost could show him, caused by the event, was one of pleasure.

"Let me see some tenderness connected with a death," said Scrooge; "or that dark chamber, Spirit, which we left just now, will be for ever present to me."

The Ghost conducted him through several streets familiar to his feet; and as they went along, Scrooge looked here and there to find himself, but nowhere was he to be seen. They entered poor Bob Cratchit's house; the dwelling he had visited before; and found the mother and the children seated round the fire.

Quiet. Very quiet. The noisy little Cratchits were as still as statues in one corner, and sat looking up at Peter, who had a book before him. The mother and her daughters were engaged in sewing. But surely they were very quiet.

"And he took a child, and set him in the midst of them."

Where had Scrooge heard those words? He had not dreamed them. The boy must have read them out, as he and the Spirit crossed the threshold. Why did he not go on?

The mother laid her work upon the table, and put her hand up to her face.

"The colour hurts my eyes," she said.

The colour? Ah, poor Tiny Tim.

"They're better now again," said Cratchit's wife. "It makes them weak by candle-light; and I wouldn't show weak eyes to your father when he comes home, for the world. It must be near his time."

"Past it rather," Peter answered, shutting up his book. "But I think he's walked a little slower than he used, these few last evenings, mother."

They were very quiet again. At last she said, and in a steady, cheerful voice, that only faltered once:

"I have known him walk with -- I have known him walk with Tiny Tim upon his shoulder, very fast indeed."

"And so have I," cried Peter. "Often."

"And so have I," exclaimed another. So had all.

"But he was very light to carry," she resumed, intent upon her work, "and his father loved him so, that it was no trouble -- no trouble. And there is your father at the door!"

She hurried out to meet him; and little Bob in his comforter -- he had need of it, poor fellow -- came in. His tea was ready for him on the hob, and they all tried who should help him to it most. Then the two young Cratchits got upon his knees and laid, each child a little cheek, against his face, as if they said, "Don't mind it, father. Don't be grieved."

Bob was very cheerful with them, and spoke pleasantly to all the family. He looked at the work upon the table, and praised the industry and speed of Mr. s. Cratchit and the girls. They would be done long before Sunday, he said.

"Sunday. You went to-day, then, Robert?" said his wife.

"Yes, my dear," returned Bob. "I wish you could have gone. It would have done you good to see how green a place it is. But you'll see it often. I promised him that I would walk there on a Sunday. My little, little child!" cried Bob. "My little child!"

He broke down all at once. He couldn't help it. If he could have helped it, he and his child would have been farther apart perhaps than they were.

He left the room, and went up-stairs into the room above, which was lighted cheerfully, and hung with Christmas. There was a chair set close beside the child, and there were signs of some one having been there, lately. Poor Bob sat down in it, and when he had thought a little and composed himself, he kissed the little face. He was reconciled to what had happened, and went down again quite happy.

They drew about the fire, and talked; the girls and mother working still. Bob told them of the extraordinary kindness of Mr. Scrooge's nephew, whom he had scarcely seen but once, and who, meeting him in the street that day, and seeing that he looked a little -- "just a little down you know," said Bob, inquired what had happened to distress him. "On which," said Bob, "for he is the pleasantest-spoken gentleman you ever heard, I told him. 'I am heartily sorry for it, Mr. Cratchit,' he said, 'and heartily sorry for your good wife.' By the bye, how he ever knew that, I don't know."

"Knew what, my dear?"

"Why, that you were a good wife," replied Bob.

"Everybody knows that," said Peter.

"Very well observed, my boy!" cried Bob. "I hope they do. 'Heartily sorry,' he said, 'for your good wife. If I can be of service to you in any way,' he said, giving me his card, 'that's where I live. Pray come to me.' Now, it wasn't," cried Bob," for the sake of anything he might be able to do for us, so much as for his kind way, that this was quite delightful. It really seemed as if he had known our Tiny Tim, and felt with us."

"I'm sure he's a good soul," said Mr. s. Cratchit.

"You would be surer of it, my dear," returned Bob, "if you saw and spoke to him. I shouldn't be at all surprised mark what I say, if he got Peter a better situation."

"Only hear that, Peter," said Mr. s. Cratchit.

"And then," cried one of the girls, "Peter will be keeping company with some one, and setting up for himself."

"Get along with you!" retorted Peter, grinning.

"It's just as likely as not," said Bob, "one of these days; though there's plenty of time for that, my dear. But however and when ever we part from one another, I am sure we shall none of us forget poor Tiny Tim -- shall we -- or this first parting that there was among us."

"Never, father!" cried they all.

"And I know," said Bob, "I know, my dears, that when we recollect how patient and how mild he was; although he was a little, little child; we shall not quarrel easily among ourselves, and forget poor Tiny Tim in doing it."

"No, never, father!" they all cried again.

"I am very happy," said little Bob, "I am very happy!"

Mr. s. Cratchit kissed him, his daughters kissed him, the two young Cratchits kissed him, and Peter and himself shook hands. Spirit of Tiny Tim, thy childish essence was from God.

"Spectre," said Scrooge, "something informs me that our parting moment is at hand. I know it, but I know not how. Tell me what man that was whom we saw lying dead."

The Ghost of Christmas Yet To Come conveyed him, as before -- though at a different time, he thought: indeed, there seemed no order in these latter visions, save that they were in the Future -- into the resorts of business men, but showed him not himself. Indeed, the Spirit did not stay for anything, but went straight on, as to the end just now desired, until besought by Scrooge to tarry for a moment.

"This courts," said Scrooge, "through which we hurry now, is where my place of occupation is, and has been for a length of time. I see the house. Let me behold what I shall be, in days to come."

The Spirit stopped; the hand was pointed elsewhere.

"The house is yonder," Scrooge exclaimed. "Why do you point away?"

The inexorable finger underwent no change.

Scrooge hastened to the window of his office, and looked in. It was an office still, but not his. The furniture was not the same, and the figure in the chair was not himself. The Phantom pointed as before.

He joined it once again, and wondering why and whither he had gone, accompanied it until they reached an iron gate. He paused to look round before entering.

A churchyard. Here, then, the wretched man whose name he had now to learn, lay underneath the ground. It was a worthy place. Walled in by houses; overrun by grass and weeds, the growth of vegetation's death, not life; choked up with too much burying; fat with repleted appetite. A worthy place!

The Spirit stood among the graves, and pointed down to One. He advanced towards it trembling. The Phantom was exactly as it had been, but he dreaded that he saw new meaning in its solemn shape.

"Before I draw nearer to that stone to which you point," said Scrooge, "answer me one question. Are these the shadows of the things that Will be, or are they shadows of things that May be, only?"

Still the Ghost pointed downward to the grave by which it stood.

"Men's courses will foreshadow certain ends, to which, if persevered in, they must lead," said Scrooge. "But if the courses be departed from, the ends will change. Say it is thus with what you show me."

The Spirit was immovable as ever.

Scrooge crept towards it, trembling as he went; and following the finger, read upon the stone of the neglected grave his own name, EBENEZER SCROOGE.

"Am I that man who lay upon the bed?" he cried, upon his knees.

The finger pointed from the grave to him, and back again.

"No, Spirit! Oh no, no!"

The finger still was there.

"Spirit!" he cried, tight clutching at its robe, "hear me. I am not the man I was. I will not be the man I must have been but for this intercourse. Why show me this, if I am past all hope?"

For the first time the hand appeared to shake.

"Good Spirit," he pursued, as down upon the ground he fell before it: "Your nature intercedes for me, and pities me. Assure me that I yet may change these shadows you have shown me, by an altered life."

The kind hand trembled.

"I will honour Christmas in my heart, and try to keep it all the year. I will live in the Past, the Present, and the Future. The Spirits of all Three shall strive within me. I will not shut out the lessons that they teach. Oh, tell me I may sponge away the writing on this stone!"

In his agony, he caught the spectral hand. It sought to free itself, but he was strong in his entreaty, and detained it. The Spirit, stronger yet, repulsed him.

Holding up his hands in a last prayer to have his fate aye reversed, he saw an alteration in the Phantom's hood and dress. It shrunk, collapsed, and dwindled down into a bedpost.

Mini-Lesson

Sometimes students wonder about whether their paper should have indents at the beginning of each paragraph, or should they skip a line instead. You will notice often that sometimes you will see one way and sometimes the other. What is correct?

In manuscript writing the industry standard is to double space each line and indent each paragraph. In friendly or informal letters such as thank you notes manuscript style is the choice to use.

In professional writing such as business letters the standard is called Blocked. All paragraphs start flush to the left and a line is skipped between each paragraph. You will note this reading is done blocked style. When the work ends flush to the right it appears from a distance that the work is done in blocks.

If you are not sure, the best thing to do is to ask your teacher which style she/he would like the paper done in, Manuscript or Blocked. Then follow the direction of your teacher.

Writing a Compare and Contrast Essay

Know your topic. Your topic is comparing 19th century England to life in your country now. That is too broad a topic so narrow it down. Some ideas might be

Transportation	Family sizes
Sleeping arrangements	Religion
Caring for the handicapped	Food
Celebrating Christmas	How meals are eaten

Go to the internet and gather some information. Make certain you include the place or places you went to in your sources.

Make an outline.

Pull your information together into two well written paragraphs, one on how they are alike and one on how they are different. Each paragraph needs a topic sentence.

You need a concluding paragraph at the end summarizing the information. You might also want to put in an opening paragraph telling the reader why you chose the topic you chose. This would make your essay more interesting.

You will note that there is more information gathered than is used. This is good. You need more information to pick from. Your outline is a tool to gather information and you will often have more than needed.

Remember to copy your url address of the source you use. In the future you will be learning how to properly cite a source and if you already know how you can do a proper citation.

Sample Essay

Professor Roundy
123456789
December 11, 2102
Assignment 14
Word count 400
//
//

Compare and Contrast Classrooms in China and Idaho

I am teaching in China and would like to compare and contrast my classrooms of China and Idaho. In some ways classrooms are very much alike. We both have desks and chairs that can be moved around. We have a computer and a projector so that all of the students can see what we put up. Both have two exits for fire safety and open up into a hallway. In these ways the classrooms are similar.

There are many contrasts between my classrooms in China and in Idaho. In Idaho I was able to design my own classroom. Most teachers do not get to do this so it was special. My father helped me and it was very nice. We do not use chalk boards in Idaho, we use white boards. I like chalk boards better and the chalk in China is a very high quality. It is difficult to find such good quality chalk in Idaho. My classroom had carpet on the floors and it made the floors warm. Although I had a projector in my classroom, I had to buy it myself because I felt it was important. If I did not buy it myself I would have to share one with all of the other teachers. Another contrast is that our classrooms are heated and are warm in Idaho. I feel badly for my students in China who have to write with cold hands but they do it willingly. In Idaho I did not have windows in my classroom and I like windows. In China the classrooms have windows so the students can benefit from fresh air and sunshine. In Idaho my classroom was big enough that we had lots of extra room to move around and we could go into groups. Many rooms in Idaho are more crowded, much more crowded than classrooms here, but I got to design my room so it had more space.

Every place in the world has different classrooms. Some are mud huts and others are new spacious centers for learning. It is not the classroom that makes the difference, however, it is the students and all of my students, both in Idaho and at SJTU are excited to learn and engaged in making their time in school count. That is what I think is the most important part of a classroom, the students.

Why Edit

When a person writes an essay the person often does not see their own errors. Your eyes become used to them and adapt. We need someone else to read our essays to find the errors we did not see. When our classmates do this it is called peer editing. Peers are the equals in your class. Many western university English professors insist that all students peer edit. One reason is to catch the mistakes the writer does not see. Also it lets you, the peer, read other essays to give you more ideas for your own writing. Lastly as you edit you may question if something is an error and discuss it with your peers and the teacher and learn more yourself about English. Your author, Professor Roundy, once had an important document to complete and had ten people edit it before it was given to the authorities who needed it.

An important part of peer editing is leaving a positive affirmation after you are done. Point out things that you liked about the essay. Were there few or no mechanical errors you could find, let the writer know. Does it read well, is it fluent, let the writer know. Most important, did it entertain you and was if interesting or entertaining to read? Write a note.

Just for fun, see if you can read this note from a study of the brain. It is an excellent example of how the brain adjusts to errors and reads right over them substituting the correct letters or words.

7H15 M3554G3
53RV35 TO PR0V3
HOW 0UR M1NDS C4N
D0 4M4Z1NG 7H1NG5!
1MPR3551V3 557H1NG5!
1N 7H3 B3G1NN1NG
17 WA5 H4RD BU7
N0W, 0N 7H15 LIN3
Y0UR M1ND 1S
R34D1NG 17
4U70M471C4LLY
W17H 0U7 3V3N
7H1NK1NG 4B0U7 17.
B3 PR0UD! 0NLY
C3R741N P30PL3 C4N
R3AD 7H15.
Y0U 4R3 0N3 0F 7H3M!

Meta Model Challenge

This lesson will have a Modal Operator of Possibility. Modal operators of possibility include can't, impossible, won't, and couldn't. To challenge it ask, Why?"

It won't be Rudolf?

Why won't it be Rudolf?

Next use your creativity to answer the question you created. This is where your writing expands.

It won't be Rudolf because the reindeer here has a black nose and Rudolf's is bright and glowing red, I know because I saw him on TV in the movie about his life.

It could be Rudolf, let me look at him again, hey, he is pulling Santa's sleigh and he has a bright red nose, I guess it is Rudolf after all.

Lesson 17: A Christmas Carol and Peer Editing

Homework Assignment

When you get your peer-edited essay back, look at the edits and comments your peers have made for you. Go back and fix any mistakes they have found. If you are not sure, ask the teacher because your peers may make a mistake and you are responsible for any errors on your paper. It is good to question and get the answer, correct it and hand it in in the next class. After you are done, edit your own essay. Make sure your work is in the layout your teacher requires. Look for typing errors. Check for mechanical errors and fluency errors, then print

Prepare for the final assessment next week where you will show what you know.

Weekly Reading

A CHRISTMAS CAROL by Charles Dickens

Stave 5: The End of It

Yes! and the bedpost was his own. The bed was his own, the room was his own. Best and happiest of all, the Time before him was his own, to make amends in!

"I will live in the Past, the Present, and the Future!" Scrooge repeated, as he scrambled out of bed. "The Spirits of all Three shall strive within me. Oh Jacob Marley! Heaven, and the Christmas Time be praised for this. I say it on my knees, old Jacob, on my knees!"

He was so fluttered and so glowing with his good intentions, that his broken voice would scarcely answer to his call. He had been sobbing violently in his conflict with the Spirit, and his face was wet with tears.

"They are not torn down!" cried Scrooge, folding one of his bed-curtains in his arms, "they are not torn down, rings and all. They are here -- I am here -- the shadows of the things that would have been, may be dispelled. They will be! I know they will."

His hands were busy with his garments all this time; turning them inside out, putting them on upside down, tearing them, mislaying them, making them parties to every kind of extravagance.

"I don't know what to do!" cried Scrooge, laughing and crying in the same breath; and making a perfect Laocoon of himself with his stockings. "I am as light as a feather, I am as happy as an angel, I am as merry as a schoolboy. I am as giddy as a drunken man. A merry Christmas to everybody! A happy New Year to all the world! Hallo here! Whoop! Hallo!"

He had frisked into the sitting-room, and was now standing there: perfectly winded.

"There's the saucepan that the gruel was in!" cried Scrooge, starting off again, and frisking round the fireplace. "There's the door, by which the Ghost of Jacob Marley entered. There's the corner where the Ghost of Christmas Present, sat. There's the window where I saw the wandering Spirits. It's all right, it's all true, it all happened. Ha haha!"

Really, for a man who had been out of practice for so many years, it was a splendid laugh, a most illustrious laugh. The father of a long, long line of brilliant laughs.

"I don't know what day of the month it is," said Scrooge. "I don't know how long I've been among the Spirits. I don't know anything. I'm quite a baby. Never mind. I don't care. I'd rather be a baby. Hallo! Whoop! Hallo here!"

He was checked in his transports by the churches ringing out the lustiest peals he had ever heard. Clash, clang, hammer; ding, dong, bell! Bell, dong, ding; hammer, clang, clash! Oh, glorious, glorious!

Running to the window, he opened it, and put out his head. No fog, no mist; clear, bright, jovial, stirring, cold; cold, piping for the blood to dance to; Golden sunlight; Heavenly sky; sweet fresh air; merry bells. Oh, glorious. Glorious!

"What's to-day?" cried Scrooge, calling downward to a boy in Sunday clothes, who perhaps had loitered in to look about him.

"Eh?" returned the boy, with all his might of wonder.

"What's to-day, my fine fellow?" said Scrooge.

"To-day?" replied the boy. "Why, Christmas Day."

"It's Christmas Day!" said Scrooge to himself. "I haven't missed it. The Spirits have done it all in one night. They can do anything they like. Of course they can. Of course they can. Hallo, my fine fellow!"

"Hallo!" returned the boy.

"Do you know the Poulterer's, in the next street but one, at the corner?" Scrooge inquired.

"I should hope I did," replied the lad.

"An intelligent boy!" said Scrooge. "A remarkable boy! Do you know whether they've sold the prize Turkey that was hanging up there -- Not the little prize Turkey: the big one?"

"What, the one as big as me?" returned the boy.

"What a delightful boy!" said Scrooge. "It's a pleasure to talk to him. Yes, my buck."

"It's hanging there now," replied the boy.

"Is it?" said Scrooge. "Go and buy it."

"Walk-er!" exclaimed the boy.

"No, no," said Scrooge, "I am in earnest. Go and buy it, and tell them to bring it here, that I may give them the direction where to take it. Come back with the man, and I'll give you a shilling. Come back with him in less than five minutes and I'll give you half-a-crown."

The boy was off like a shot. He must have had a steady hand at a trigger who could have got a shot off half so fast.

"I'll send it to Bon Cratchit's!" whispered Scrooge, rubbing his hands, and splitting with a laugh. "He shan't know who sends it. It's twice the size of Tiny Tim. Joe Miller never made such a joke as sending it to Bob's will be!"

The hand in which he wrote the address was not a steady one, but write it he did, somehow, and went down-stairs to open the street door, ready for the coming of the poulterer's man. As he stood there, waiting his arrival, the knocker caught his eye.

"I shall love it, as long as I live!" cried Scrooge, patting it with his hand. "I scarcely ever looked at it before. What an honest expression it has in its face. It's a wonderful knocker. -- Here's the Turkey. Hallo! Whoop! How are you? Merry Christmas!"

It was a Turkey! He never could have stood upon his legs, that bird. He would have snapped them short off in a minute, like sticks of sealing-wax.

"Why, it's impossible to carry that to Camden Town," said Scrooge. "You must have a cab."

The chuckle with which he said this, and the chuckle with which he paid for the Turkey, and the chuckle with which he paid for the cab, and the chuckle with which he recompensed the boy, were only to be exceeded by the chuckle with which he sat down breathless in his chair again, and chuckled till he cried.

Shaving was not an easy task, for his hand continued to shake very much; and shaving requires attention, even when you don't dance while you are at it. But if he had cut the end of his nose off, he would have put a piece of sticking-plaister over it, and been quite satisfied.

He dressed himself all in his best, and at last got out into the streets. The people were by this time pouring forth, as he had seen them with the Ghost of Christmas Present; and walking with his hands behind him, Scrooge regarded every one with a delighted smile. He looked so irresistibly pleasant, in a word, that three or four good-humoured fellows said, "Good morning, sir. A merry Christmas to you." And Scrooge said often afterwards, that of all the blithe sounds he had ever heard, those were the blithest in his ears.

He had not gone far, when coming on towards him he beheld the portly gentleman, who had walked into his counting-house the day before, and said, "Scrooge and Marley's, I believe." It sent a pang across his heart to think how this old gentleman would look upon him when they met; but he knew what path lay straight before him, and he took it.

"My dear sir," said Scrooge, quickening his pace, and taking the old gentleman by both his hands. "How do you do. I hope you succeeded yesterday. It was very kind of you. A merry Christmas to you, sir!"

"Mr. Scrooge?"

"Yes," said Scrooge. "That is my name, and I fear it may not be pleasant to you. Allow me to ask your pardon. And will you have the goodness" -- here Scrooge whispered in his ear.

"Lord bless me!" cried the gentleman, as if his breath were taken away. "My dear Mr. Scrooge, are you serious?"

"If you please," said Scrooge. "Not a farthing less. A great many back-payments are included in it, I assure you. Will you do me that favour?"

"My dear sir," said the other, shaking hands with him. "I don't know what to say to such munificence."

"Don't say anything please," retorted Scrooge. "Come and see me. Will you come and see me?"

"I will!" cried the old gentleman. And it was clear he meant to do it.

"Thank you," said Scrooge. "I am much obliged to you. I thank you fifty times. Bless you!"

He went to church, and walked about the streets, and watched the people hurrying to and fro, and patted children on the head, and questioned beggars, and looked down into the kitchens of houses, and up to the windows, and found that everything could yield him pleasure. He had never dreamed that any walk -- that anything -- could give him so much happiness. In the afternoon he turned his steps towards his nephew's house.

He passed the door a dozen times, before he had the courage to go up and knock. But he made a dash, and did it:

"Is your master at home, my dear?" said Scrooge to the girl. Nice girl. Very.

"Yes, sir."

"Where is he, my love?" said Scrooge.

"He's in the dining-room, sir, along with mistress. I'll show you up-stairs, if you please."

"Thank you. He knows me," said Scrooge, with his hand already on the dining-room lock. "I'll go in here, my dear."

He turned it gently, and sidled his face in, round the door. They were looking at the table (which was spread out in great array); for these young housekeepers are always nervous on such points, and like to see that everything is right.

"Fred!" said Scrooge.

Dear heart alive, how his niece by marriage started. Scrooge had forgotten, for the moment, about her sitting in the corner with the footstool, or he wouldn't have done it, on any account.

"Why bless my soul!" cried Fred," who's that?"

"It's I. Your uncle Scrooge. I have come to dinner. Will you let me in, Fred?"

Let him in! It is a mercy he didn't shake his arm off. He was at home in five minutes. Nothing could be heartier. His niece looked just the same. So did Topper when he came. So did the plump sister when she came. So did every one when they came. Wonderful party, wonderful games, wonderful unanimity, won-der-ful happiness!

But he was early at the office next morning. Oh he was early there. If he could only be there first, and catch Bob Cratchit coming late! That was the thing he had set his heart upon.

And he did it; yes, he did. The clock struck nine. No Bob. A quarter past. No Bob. He was full eighteen minutes and a half behind his time. Scrooge sat with his door wide open, that he might see him come into the Tank.

His hat was off, before he opened the door; his comforter too. He was on his stool in a jiffy; driving away with his pen, as if he were trying to overtake nine o'clock.

"Hallo," growled Scrooge, in his accustomed voice, as near as he could feign it. "What do you mean by coming here at this time of day?"

"I'm very sorry, sir," said Bob. "I *am* behind my time."

"You are?" repeated Scrooge. "Yes. I think you are. Step this way, if you please."

"It's only once a year, sir," pleaded Bob, appearing from the Tank. "It shall not be repeated. I was making rather merry yesterday, sir."

"Now, I'll tell you what, my friend," said Scrooge, "I am not going to stand this sort of thing any longer. And therefore," he continued, leaping from his stool, and giving Bob such a dig in the waistcoat that he staggered back into the Tank again; "and therefore I am about to raise your salary."

Bob trembled, and got a little nearer to the ruler. He had a momentary idea of knocking Scrooge down with it, holding him, and calling to the people in the court for help and a strait-waistcoat.

"A merry Christmas, Bob," said Scrooge, with an earnestness that could not be mistaken, as he clapped him on the back. "A merrier Christmas, Bob, my good fellow, than I have given you for many a year. I'll raise your salary, and endeavour to assist your struggling family, and we will discuss your affairs this very afternoon, over a Christmas bowl of smoking bishop, Bob. Make up the fires, and buy another coal-scuttle before you dot another *i*, Bob Cratchit!"

Scrooge was better than his word. He did it all, and infinitely more; and to Tiny Tim, who did not die, he was a second father. He became as good a friend, as good a master, and as good a man, as the good old city knew, or any other good old city, town, or borough, in the good old world. Some people laughed to see the alteration in him, but he let them laugh, and little heeded them; for he was wise enough to know that nothing ever happened on this globe, for good, at which some people did not have their fill of laughter in the outset; and knowing that such as these would be blind anyway, he thought it quite as well that they should wrinkle up their eyes in grins, as have the malady in less attractive forms. His own heart laughed: and that was quite enough for him.

He had no further intercourse with Spirits, but lived upon the Total Abstinence Principle, ever afterwards; and it was always said of him, that he knew how to keep Christmas well, if any man alive possessed the knowledge. May that be truly said of us, and all of us! And so, as Tiny Tim observed, God Bless Us, Every One!

Lesson 18: A Christmas Carol and Final Review

Homework

None.

Weekly Reading

Reminders for your assessment day:

* Check to make certain your name is on your test.
* Put your student number on both sides of test.
* Check to make certain you answered all questions. Go back and check.
* Lose points on comprehension if not on both sides.

Sample

None

Section 2
Practice for In-Class Writing

Lesson 1: Lesson of Introduction

Class work

Today you will embark on a new adventure, that of creative writing in English. It is up to you to go through the door.

Discuss It

The door of opportunity won't open unless you do some pushing. ~ Author Unknown

Fix It

bucky beaver eight beverly bears bananas so
angy beverly bear eight bucky beavers bark

Expand It

the girl sat.

Lesson 2: Character Sketch

Class work

In this lesson you will hear the story of the dolphins and the power of positive affirmations. Your assignment will include a character sketch.

Discuss It

Every child born has innate goodness. – Chinese Proverb

Fix It

in san diego california the dolphins jumped through an hoop then caught a ball on they'er noses at seeWorld

(hint, World should be capitalized. It is the the middle of a word but it is a proper noun and that is how the business chose to write the name of the business.)

There are 9 errors.

Expand It

the fish

Lesson 3: Obituaries

Class work

Today's lesson is about Neil Armstrong, the first man to walk on the moon. If you are not able to come to class, look up information about Mr. Armstrong on the internet before you start your assignment. For the practice section we will look at the famous American President Abraham Lincoln. He is especially well-known throughout the world for freeing the Black Americans from slavery.

Discuss It

As I would not be a slave, so I would not be a master. --- Abraham Lincoln

Fix It

abraham lincoln did not believe that slavery should spread in the usa he believed african-americans should get the rights granted in the declaration of independence: life liberty the pursuit of happiness

There are 15 errors.

Expand It

Lincoln was president

Lesson 4: Giving Directions

Class work

Today you will be writing in first person. You may use the first person words ***I, me and my***. We will focus on giving directions. Good directions can help you get where you want to go.

Discuss It

Write about a time in your life when you got lost. Write it in first person using words such as I, me, and my.

Fix It

when i was 8 we moved two a knew house and i walked
home from school and took the wrong road and got lost and
my mother got worried and came out too find me

There are about ten errors in this sentence depending on how you correct it.

Expand It

lost

Lesson 5: Writing Directions to Do a Thing

Class work

As students when we work on essays we want to use a plethora of descriptive words to make our essay interesting. We want to paint a picture with words to enliven the imagination of the reader. Writing directions is very different. The beautiful and poetic words of an essay entangle the reader of directions. Directions need to be concise and easy to read with no extraneous words. This week we will practice this style of writing.

Discuss It

Talent is cheaper than table salt. What separates the talented individual from the successful one is a lot of hard work. ---Stephen King

Fix It

directions from the east junior high to big valley park

first exit the school though the main doors
second go east to h street
third cross the street and keep going straight east
go about 1/2 km
now you are at big valley park
if you need help text i at 456-7890

There are 18 errors

Expand It

Needing help

Lesson 6: Descriptive Essay

Class work

This lesson will wrap up our practice of writing directions in a concise manner. In this lesson you get to share about your home town or a town or city you have visited. Paint a picture that will make the reader want to visit the place you call home.

Discuss It

I look up to the sky and see the big, bright moon. I gaze down and think about my far way homeland. ~ Chinese anonymous

Fix It

how to write an essay about your hometown

staart with whatever makes your hometown special to you
pretend you are talking two a stranger
paint an word picture of the special place
remember that a essay is an short written works
make the title creative so people will want to read the essay
when you are done proof-read you work

Expand It

Sight to see

Lesson 7: The Friendly Letter

Class work

Today you will fix titles and discuss the power of the written word through the friendly letter. This is often a favorite lesson because it brings back good memories of someone you love.

Discuss It

But those who are looking ahead down the road see a different trend, a new curve in the road that may turn us toward a renaissance of the written word, a triumph of text, a return to writing. We have known for centuries that written communication tends to be more thoughtful, more concise, more careful, and more efficient that the mere spoken words that emerge seemingly without benefit of reason from our mouths. And yet we have maintained in our schools and colleges an oral culture of communication -- we speak and listen in our classrooms much more often than we write and read.

~ Jim Lengel, Education and Technology Consultant, 04/24/2006

Fix It

Fix these titles

a history of letter writing

collection of letters by alyssa b slater

letters of abraham lincoln during the war years

There are 16 errors.

Expand It

writing

Lesson 8: Formal Emails

Class work

It is important in this modern time of technology that students know how to put together a good email. Students know how to text from an early age and shoot each other quick emails and tweets but there is arising a need to know how to put together a more formal email.

Discuss It

Technology gives us power, but it does not and cannot tell us how to use that power. Thanks to technology, we can instantly communicate across the world, but it still doesn't help us know what to say.

~ Jonathan Sacks

Fix It

407 east pacific
santa cruz california 93265
8th july 2015

dear friends

this year is a fourtieth birthday of the founding of nlp   us would like two have an big celebration and hope you will come   invited will be nlp persons form all over the world   suzi smith and judith delozier will be theyre   us hope that john grinder and richard bandler   the founders of nlp   will be in attendance

sincerely yours

r dilts

There are about 47 mistakes

Expand It

internet

Lesson 9: Western Culture: Halloween

Class work

This lesson will look at western culture with a popular minor holiday, Halloween.

Discuss It

You are going to have a Halloween party. How will you decorate for it? Remember only 5 minutes.

Fix It

five pumpkins and an witch

five little pumpkins sitting in an fence
an which came riding bye
ho ho ho ill take you all
and make i an pumpkin pi

There are about 22 errors.

Expand It

pumpkin

Challenge It

You can't wear a mask on Halloween.

Lesson 10: Poetry

Class work

Have you ever taken on a challenge that seemed impossible and then did it? Today we will look at that very topic.

Discuss It

It Couldn't Be Done
BY EDGAR ALBERT GUEST
Somebody said that it couldn't be done
    But he with a chuckle replied
That "maybe it couldn't," but he would be one
    Who wouldn't say so till he'd tried.
So he buckled right in with the trace of a grin
    On his face. If he worried he hid it.
He started to sing as he tackled the thing
    That couldn't be done, and he did it!

Write about a time when you had an experience that illustrates this quote or a time when someone you know had an experience that illustrates this quote.

Challenge It

It is necessary to do the thing that cannot be done.

Write a question challenging the Model Operator of Necessity

Fix It

their are thousands two tell you it cannot be done
    they're are thousands too prophesy failure
there are thousands to point out two you 1 bye 1
    the dangers that wait to assail you
but just buckle in with a bit of a grin
    just take of you   coat and go two it
just start in two sing as you tackle a thing
    that "cannot be done " and youll do it

This is the third stanza of the poem **It Couldn't Be Done** BY EDGAR ALBERT GUEST.
It is missing 2 periods, 5 commas, and 1 semicolon
There are 30 errors.

Expand It

Impossible

Lesson 11: Writing a Pro/Con Essay

Class work

This week we will look at an issue from both sides. The issue discussed in the classwork is the One Child Policy in China.

Discuss It

"If a son is uneducated, his dad is to blame." ~Chinese Proverb

Fix It

the family is giong two town tells us it is an specific or definate family
the is a definate article and specifies

a family is goind to town do not define the family
a is a indefinate article

There are 15 errors

Expand It

child

Challenge It

Challenge It Meta Model: Model Operators of Possibility

Modal operators of possibility include can't, impossible, won't, couldn't, and wouldn't

It is impossible to love more than one child.

Lesson 12: Copyrights

Class work

This lesson begins to cover copyright issues. It is important to be honest in all of our work. We will also address virtues and honesty is an important virtue to cultivate in our lives.

Discuss It

"Honesty is the first chapter in the book of Wisdom."---Thomas Jefferson

Fix It

if our words are not consistent with our actions they will never bee herd above the thunder of us deeds ---h burke peterson

There are 11 errors.

Expand It

honesty

Challenge It

Presupposition:

X is assumed true so Y is also true.

All university students are smart so there is no cheating going on.

Lesson 13: Thanksgiving and a Christmas Carol

Class work

In both the United States and Canada the autumn season is a season of harvest and thanksgiving. Both countries have a day set aside for Thanksgiving. It is a family celebration.

Discuss It

Thanksgiving Day comes, by statute, once a year; to the honest man it comes as frequently as the heart of gratitude will allow. - Edward Sandford Martin

Fix It

four each new morning with it's lites
four rest & shelter of the nights
four health & food, four love & friends
four everything, thy goodness sends
- ralph waldo emerson

There are 19 errors in the poem above by the famous poet, Emerson.

Expand It

gratitude

Challenge It

Write a challenge question for the Meta Model pattern Mind Reading or The Crystal ball.

I know you want to have turkey for Thanksgiving Dinner!

Lesson 14: A Christmas Carol and Character Analysis

Class work

You will continue your reading of Dickens' A Christmas Carol and do a character analysis on a character in the book of your choice from the list given.

Discuss It

By selflessness you fulfill yourself. By generously giving you gather riches. Ralph Marston

Fix It

"there is an magnet in your heart that will attract true friends   That magnet was unselfishness, thinking of others 1st...when you learn two live four others, they will live four you." ~ paramahansa yogananda

10 errors

Expand It

A person I know who is selfless is__________ because __________

One sentence only

Challenge It

Challenge the Meta model pattern, "I don't know."

I don't know why my mother is so unselfish.

Lesson 15: A Christmas Carol and Outlines

Class work

Your final project will be a compare and contrast essay. You will begin that essay with this week's lesson learning the skill of making an outline. This will be a small research project.

Discuss It

'Any sufficiently advanced technology is indistinguishable from magic.' -Arthur C. Clarke

Fix It

us live on an society exquisitely dependent in sceince & technology, in witch hardly anyone nose anything about science & technology - carl sagan

13 errors watch for homonyms and a spelling error.

Expand It

technology

Challenge It

Challenge the universal qualifier.

Using technology is always the better way.

Lesson 16: A Christmas Carol and Compare and Contrast Essays

Class work

In this lesson we will think about our association with computers and the internet. Is it an advantage or is it an addicting curse to mankind. We will also review the format of a friendly latter. This work is in preparation for your final test.

Discuss It

We are so used to multitasking, we are so addicted to overachieving that we forget that real happiness lies in simple things that take place in the present. --Sumesh Nair

Fix It

In western countries children often write a letter to Santa Claus telling him about the good things they have done during the year. Of course children do not really believe in Santa Claus coming to their home and know that their parents are really the source of all of the gifts and presents. Still it gives them a moment to reflect on the good they have done and to remember how it felt to do something good. It provides a draw towards doing more good the next year.

dec 11 2018
dear mr claus
upon reflecting on my year i can sum my behavior up in one word
good kind and loving I no i am deserving t please bring me the latest
iphone and a computer and a watch and a ipad I promise to take care of
them carefully
your bestest friend
molly

ps i love you

There are several was to correct this. There are about 25-30 errors depending on how you fix it.

Expand It

addictions

Challenge It

Challenge the modal operator of possibility.

I will not give up the use of my smart phone for even a day.

Lesson 17: A Christmas Carol and Peer Editing

Class work

Our lesson will include reviewing friendly letter skills and learning a few facts about the Western Holiday of Christmas. This holiday is one of the biggest holidays of the year and is both a religious holiday with deep meaning to Christians, and also a large commercial enterprise where a business can make or break their fiscal financial year. Others also celebrate the season beside Christians including Hanukah for the Jews worldwide, Kwanza for those of African American descent, the New Year for many calendars and the Winter Solstice.

Discuss It

Write a friendly (informal) letter to your mother or another telling her what you are doing in school.

This is a practice in friendly letter skills.

Fix It

st nicholas was a fourth century christian who is known for his quiet good deeds such as putting coins in shoes of poor persons over the centurys she became the model four st nick or santa claus

There are about 16 errors.

Expand It

Santa Claus

Challenge It

It can't be St Nick.

Lesson 18: A Christmas Carol and Final Review

Class work

This lesson will be your final test. Below is information and helps for you to do well on the final. Below the information is a sample similar to what your final will look like if you would like to have a practice run Your authors wish you good luck and trust you have learned a lot about writing and have expanded your writing with creativity.

Discuss It

There will be a topic to discuss on your exam. You will have five minutes. Take a few seconds to organize your thoughts first then put them on paper.

Fix It

There will be a fix it that will be similar to others you have had in your classwork. Review the areas you had difficulty on to prepare for this section of the exam.

Expand It

You will have a word to expand into a well-formed sentence. Remember to use adjectives and adverbs to give your sentence clarity. This is a sentence you make up yourself so it does not have to be true so be creative.

Challenge It

You will have a Meta Model challenge from the patterns you have learned this term. You will need to question that pattern in a simple sentence and then creatively answer your challenge. We have learned:

- Model Operators Necessity
- Model Operators of Possibility
- Universal Qualifiers
- Presuppositions
- Mind Reading or The Crystal ball
- I don't know

Section 3

Selected Answers for In-Class Writing

Lesson 1: Lesson of Introduction

Discuss It

Check to see if you indented your paragraphs. Essays are usually indented.

Fix It

Bucky Beaver ate Beverly Bear's bananas, so angry Beverly Bear ate Bucky Beaver's bark. Bucky Beaver and Beverly Bear are names and so they are proper nouns.

Expand It

The girl sat.

This is your opportunity to be creative. Here is an example of a very good sentence.

The sweet little girl in the red dress sat and pensively waited until her turn to perform in the talent show at her school.

Lesson 2: Character Sketch

Discuss It

Every child born, has innate goodness. – Chinese Proverb

Check to see that you used the formal word child or children, not the slang term kid or kids.

Fix It

In San Diego, California, the dolphins jumped though a hoop then caught a ball on their noses at SeaWorld.

Expand It

I ate the fish for dinner.

This is not well expanded and would get few points.

Lesson 3: Obituaries

Discuss It

As I would not be a slave, so I would not be a master. --- Abraham Lincoln
Check your essay for a good opening statement.

Fix It

Abraham Lincoln did not believe that slavery should spread in the USA. He believed African-Americans should get the rights granted in the Declaration of Independence: life, liberty, and the pursuit of happiness.

Expand It

Here is an example of a well-done sentence.

During the time that Abraham Lincoln was the United States President most black people were slaves and the European people did not think they were entirely human but were below the human species and could be treated much as animals.

Lesson 4: Giving Directions

Discuss It

Write about a time in your life when you got lost. Write it in first person using words such as I, me, and my.

Check your essay. Did you write it in first person? Did you use an original story?

Fix It

when i was 8 we moved two a knew house and i walked home from school and took the wrong road and got lost and my mother got worried and came out too find me

When I was eight we moved to a new house and I walked home from school. I took the wrong road and got lost. My mother got worried and came out to find me.

This is only one of several ways to correct this passage.

Expand It

This is an example of a very poor expansion. It is not on topic, has few words, and there is a grammar error, "me" should be "my."

I found me watch.

Lesson 5: Writing Directions to Do a Thing

Discuss It

Talent is cheaper than table salt. What separates the talented individual from the successful one is a lot of hard work. --- Stephen King

Your essay should tell about someone you know, including yourself, who has worked hard to develop a talent.

Fix It

Directions from East Junior High to Big Valley Park

First exit the school through the main doors.

Second go east to H Street.

Third cross the street and keep going straight east, go about ½ km.

Now you are at Big Valley Park.

If you need help, text me at 456-7890

You could also use 1st, 2nd, and 3rd.

You could also make the sentence in the third section into two complete sentences.

Expand It

This is a well expanded sentence.

I am desperately needing help to get all of the essays graded before the next class as I want the students to learn from their errors, not learn their errors.

Lesson 6: Descriptive Essay

Discuss It

Check your essay for a closing statement that ties into the opening to make your essay complete like a circle.

Fix It

How to Write an Essay About Your Hometown (some people would say not to capitalize about)

Start with whatever makes your hometown special to you.
Pretend you are talking to a stranger.
Paint a work picture of the special place.
Remember that an essay is a short written work.
Make your title creative so people will want to read the essay.
When you are done, proof-read your work.

Expand It

A well-expanded example.

If you were lucky enough to visit Rupert, Idaho, a sight to see is the Rupert Town Square with the first water well in the middle and which is surrounded by historical buildings such as the old bank and the old dance hall.

Lesson 7: The Friendly Letter

Discuss It

You should have addressed speaking and listening, and compared or contrasted them to writing and reading.

Fix It

A History of Letter Writing

Collection of Letters by Alyssa B. Slater

Letters of Abraham Lincoln During the War Years

There are 16 errors.

Expand It

An expanded sentence example.

Writing things down has been the secret to keeping history and helping us as a world not to repeat the mistakes of the past.

Lesson 8: Formal Emails

Discuss It

Check your short essay for spacing after periods and commas. The rule is one space after a comma and one space after a period. In the days of typewriters it was always two spaces after a period but with the advent of the computer more and more people are using just one space; this is now standard.

Fix It

407 East Pacific
Santa Cruz, California 93265
July 8, 2015

Dear Friends,

This year is the fortieth birthday of the founding of NLP. We would like to have a big celebration and hope you will come. Invited will be NLP people from all over the world. Suzi Smith and Judith Delozier will be there. We hope that John Grinder and Richard Bandler, the founders of NLP, will be in attendance.

Sincerely yours,
R. Dilts

Expand It

Here is an example for you.

When my internet connection is really slow I feel frustrated because I enjoy surfing the net and getting the information I need quickly, not like years ago when getting information meant a trip to the library and many hours at the card catalogue and the periodicals indexes.

Lesson 9: Western Culture: Halloween

Discuss It

You are going to have a Halloween party. How will you decorate for it? Remember only 5 minutes.

This essay should be in first person. Look for me, my, and I.

Fix It

Five Pumpkins and a Witch

Five little pumpkins sitting on a fence,
A witch came riding by,
"Ho, ho, ho, I'll take you all
And make me a pumpkin pie."

There are about 22 errors.

Expand It

In my garden a have a pumpkin patch were I grow all sizes of pumpkins including, to my delight, some large enough for the small grandchildren to stand in.

Challenge It

A challenge question: Why can't I wear a mask on Halloween?

A creative answer: You can't wear a mask because the party will be in a school and it is against fire safety codes to wear a mask in school buildings.

Lesson 10: Poetry

Discuss It

Check, did you write about your own or someone you know's experience that illustrates this quote?

Challenge It

Why is it necessary to do that thing that cannot be done? What would happen if I didn't?

Fix It

There are thousands to tell you it cannot be done,
    There are thousands to prophesy failure,
There are thousands to point out to you one by one,
    The dangers that wait to assail you.
But just buckle in with a bit of a grin,
    Just take off your coat and go to it;
Just start in to sing as you tackle the thing
    That "cannot be done," and you'll do it.

This is the third stanza of the poem **It Couldn't Be Done** BY EDGAR ALBERT GUEST. (PUBLIC DOMAIN)

Expand It

The author tries to make it impossible for the students to find all of the errors in some of the "fix It's" yet invariably someone finds them all, especially if it is a group working together and pooling their knowledge

Lesson 11: Writing a Pro/Con Essay

Discuss It

Check your essay for grammar errors. Count the words. Are you writing more words in five minutes than when you started?

Fix It

"The family is going to town," tells us it is a specific or definite family.
"The" is a definite article and specifies.

"A family is going to town," does not define the family.
"A" is an indefinite article.

Expand It

Here is an example.

Hopping and skipping down the street, the small child sang, "I'm happy, so happy" as she celebrated her birthday.

Challenge It

Question: Is it really impossible to love more than one child.

A Reply: I have five children and I love them all dearly, my love expanded each time another child came into our family whether it was my own flesh and blood or a foster child, the umbrella of love expanded to cover them all.

Lesson 12: Copyrights

Discuss It

Your essay should have at least one example to support your topic.

Fix It

If our words are not consistent with our actions, they will never be heard above the thunder of our deeds. –H. Burke Peterson

Expand It

As we put together essays we should remember to site our sources and give credit to others for their work for that is the honest thing to do.

Challenge It

Sample question: Is it true that smart people never cheat?

Sample answer: Just because students are in the university does not mean there are honest, some may have cheated their way into the university.

Lesson 13: Thanksgiving and a Christmas Carol

Discuss It

Check your essay for a good opening statement that catches the reader and helps him want to read more.

Fix It

For each new morning with its lights,
For rest and shelter of the nights,
For health and food, for love and friends,
For everything, Thy goodness sends.
--Ralph Waldo Emerson

Expand It

Sample expanded sentence

I have a deep sense of gratitude as I look around me and see the beauty of nature and I wonder at the sense of helpfulness that I see exhibited consistently day after day by the good people of the world and it makes me glad that I am alive.

Challenge It

Sample question: How do you know we are having turkey, do you have a crystal ball.

Sample answer: I don't have a crystal ball but I did meet your mother at the store yesterday and she was buying a turkey and told me it was for your Thanksgiving feast.

Lesson 14: A Christmas Carol and Character Analysis

Discuss It

Check your essay for advanced vocabulary. Have you had the courage to use a word that is new to you?

Fix It

"There is a magnet in your heart that will attract true friends. That magnet is unselfishness, thinking of others first...when you learn to live for others, they will live for you." ~ Paramahansa Yogananda

(If you did not put in quote marks that is ok. They can be "understood" because the author follows.

Expand It

A person I know who is selfless is my mother because she was invited to go to Julliard School of Music but chose instead to stay home and raise us children.

Challenge It

Sample question: How do you know your mother is unselfish?

Sample answer: Julliard School of Music is world famous and if she had gone there when she was invited, her musical career would have made her famous but she chose to stay with us instead and says she never regretted it.

Lesson 15: A Christmas Carol and Outlines

Discuss It

Check your essay for punctuation. Has good punctuation become a habit for you?

Fix It

We live in a society exquisitely dependent on science and technology, in which hardly anyone knows anything about science and technology. -Carl Sagan

Expand It

Sample: I grew up before technology took off and can remember my university had the only computer in the state of Idaho and it was huge, about 3 feet wide, four feet tall and five feet long.

Challenge It

Sample question: Why is technology always the better way?

Sample answer: Actually technology is not always better, for example scientists worked hard to develop a pen that would write in space and it cost a million dollars, yet while they were developing it what did they use but an ordinary pencil. (the pen, sold by Fisher Space Pen Company, sold for $2.95)

Lesson 16: A Christmas Carol and Compare and Contrast Essays

Discuss It

Did you address in your essay how happiness can be the little things?

Fix It

December 11, 2018

Dear Mr. Claus,

Upon reflecting on my year I can sum my behavior up in just a few words, kind, good and loving. I know I am deserving, too. Please bring me the latest iPhone, a computer, a watch and an iPad. I promise to take care of them carefully.

Your best friend,

Molly

P. S. I love you.

There are several ways to correct this. There are about 25-30 errors depending on how you fix it.

Expand It

Because the internet can constantly stimulate the brain, scientists are adding internet usage to the list of addictions known to man

Challenge It

Sample question: What would happen if you did give up the use of your smart phone for a day?

Sample answer: I guess I could give up my smart phone for a day if I got to spend the day with my family doing something special.

Lesson 17: A Christmas Carol and Peer Editing

Discuss It

Check your letter and make certain you followed all of the guidelines for a friendly letter including the correct spacing, indenting and comma usage.

Fix It

St. Nicholas was a fourth century Christian who was known for his quiet, good deeds such as putting coins in shoes of poor people. Over the centuries he became the model for St. Nick or Santa Claus.

Expand It

The imaginary old man who visits every child on Christmas Eve giving out gifts and toys is called Santa Claus.

Challenge It

Sample question: If it isn't St. Nick, who can it be?

Sample Answer: It is our neighbor, Mr. Halverson, dressed up as St. Nick to surprise the children who are missing their daddy who has to work this Christmas season far from home on the oil rig.

Lesson 18: A Christmas Carol and Final Review

Discuss It

There will be a topic to discuss on your exam. You will have five minutes. Take a few seconds to organize your thoughts first then put them on paper.

Fix It

There will be a fix it that will be similar to others you have had in your classwork. Review the areas you had difficulty on to prepare for this section of the exam.

Expand It

You will have a word to expand into a well-formed sentence. Remember to use adjectives and adverbs to give your sentence clarity. This is a sentence you make up yourself so it does not have to be true, so be creative.

Challenge It

You will have a Meta Model challenge from the patterns you have learned this term. You will need to question that pattern in a simple sentence and then creatively answer your challenge. We have learned:

- Model Operators Necessity
- Model Operators of Possibility
- Universal Qualifiers
- Presuppositions
- Mind Reading or The Crystal ball
- I don’t know

Sample Test A.	
Challenge it	Everyone hated Santa Sample question: Is there someone who liked Santa Sample answer: Actually most children love Santa but sometimes little babies are afraid of him because of his bright clothes, beard, and loud laugh.
Expand it	Santa Claus I have a friend who likes to dress up as Santa Claus and go to the houses of people who are in distress and need cheering up as he did when my daughter got a divorce just before Christmas and had no money for gifts for her children.
Fix it	201 Candy Cane Lane North Pole 00001 December 15, 2019 Dear University Student, You have studied hard this term and now you have your final test. I know you are a good student and will do your best. I hope that you can spend time with your family as families are the most important unit of society and of our lives. Families bring us happiness. Sincerely, *Santa Claus* P.S. Mr. s. Claus sends you her love. She is baking cookies for me.
Discuss it 5 minutes only	What part of the book, A Christmas Carol, did you like best? Why? Proof read your essay looking for errors.
Show you know	Make a LLA for Santa. You do not need complete sentences. You do need to use your imagination!

.

Neurological Level Alignment

		Santa
Environment	Answers when and where	All over the world
Behavior	Answers ***What?***	Leaves candy and toys for good girls and boys
Capability	Answers ***How?***	Is capable of making others happy
Beliefs and values	Answers ***why***	Believes that every good girl and boy deserves a special treat at Christmas
Identity	Answers **Who** am I ?	I am Santa Claus, a good person who loves children
Purpose	Answers “For Whom or what?”	I work for all of the children in the world giving them a special Christmas.

How did you do? Are you ready for the final?

Sources

Blanchard, Ben. (Editing by Ron Popeski). China slams "distorted" View of Copyright Piracy Problem. *Reuters*. Reuters.com. *11* November 2012. Web. November 12, 2012. <http://www.reuters.com/article/2012/11/11/us-china-congress-piracy-idUSBRE8AA04620121111>

Bynner, Witter. Fruit Poem: A Lover. Fruit Poems. *Taste Arts Inc.* 2008-2011. Web. 18 August 2014.< http://www.tastearts.com/tag/fruit-poems/>

"Cherish Your Memories." *Elegant Memorials*. Elegant Memorials.com. 2012. Web. 19 September 2012. <http://elegantmemorials.com/funeral-program-templates>

Dickens, Charles. A Christmas Carol. *Chapman & Hall*. 1843.

Dilts, Robert and Judith Delozier. Encyclopedia on Systemic NLP and NLP New Coding. NLP University Press.

Frost, Robert. The Road Not Taken. *Poem Hunter.com*. Web. 18 August 2014. <http://poemhunter.com/poem/the-road-not-taken/>

Guest, Edgar E. It Couldn't Be Done. *Poetry Foundation.* Poetry Foundation.org. CR 2014. Web. 23 September 2014. <http://www.poetryfoundation.org/poem/173579>

Lengel, Jim. "Teaching with Technology." *Power to Learn. © Copyright 2014 CSC Holdings, LLC. Web. 13 August 2014. <http://www.powertolearn.com/articles/teaching_with_technology/article.shtml?ID=22>*

McKane, Ruth Christie & Richard. To My Wife.

Microsoft Clip Art Collection. Used with permission from Microsoft.

Oleson, Alexa. Chinese Think Tank Urges End to One-child Policy *Associated Press.* 31 October 2012. Web. 2 November 2012. <http://finance.yahoo.com/news/chinese-think-tank-urges-end-one-child-policy-074125915.html?soc_src=copy>

Technology Tip Number 170. 180 Technology tips. © 2006- 180TechTips.com. Web. 13 November 2012. <http://www.180techtips.com/170.html>

The Purdue Owl. Purdue U Writing Lab, 2010. Web. 13 August 2014

http://www.memory.loc.gov/ammem/dihtml/diessay6.html

http://en.wikipedia.org/wiki/Dance_in_China

www.ingramcontent.com/pod-product-compliance
Ingram Content Group UK Ltd.
Pitfield, Milton Keynes, MK11 3LW, UK
UKHW050144280726
14058UKWH00006B/826